PORTRAIT OF
JESUS

PORTRAIT OF
JESUS

ALAN T. DALE

Illustrated by Trevor Stubley

MAYFLOWER BOOKS

First American Edition

All rights reserved under International and Pan American Copyright Convention. Published in the United States by Mayflower Books, Inc., New York, New York 10022. Originally published in England by: Oxford University Press, Oxford

Library of Congress Catalogue Card Number: 78–40196
ISBN 0 8317 7091 0

Manufactured in Great Britain

A word before you begin

This book is really written in answer to a question.

When I have been talking about Jesus and pointing out that the gospels are not 'brief biographies' or 'photographs' of Jesus but 'portraits' of him, somebody every now and then has turned to me and said 'Well, what's *your* portrait of Jesus?' On such occasions I could only give hints of what my portrait of him would be like – rough out a charcoal sketch, as it were – and make a hesitant promise that perhaps one day I would paint my portrait of Jesus properly. Here, then, at long last is my portrait of Jesus. This is how I think of him.

I had better say something about how I have gone about it, so that you can see why I have done what I have done.

The gospels are not straightforward histories. They are much richer than that. When we pick up a gospel and begin reading it, we are actually listening to the friends of Jesus talking to one another, and talking some time – ten? fifty? years – after the events they are discussing. The stories about Jesus we find there must have been told and argued about again and again. We can note the differences between the accounts of what Jesus did or said as Mark and Matthew and Luke have put them down. The argument that went on was not just about what had actually happened, but about what it all meant for them and the whole world.

We sometimes wish we could cross-examine those early friends of Jesus and ask them questions about Jesus *we* would like to ask – questions they never seem to be bothered about themselves. We are sure that we would be able to find out the truth about Jesus that way. I wonder. 'Well,' you might say, 'weren't there people still alive who had lived in Palestine when Jesus did?' I am not sure that that kind of information would help us as much as we think it would. Perhaps listening to his friends talking – as we have to – will help us more. Rudyard Kipling has written about his days as a newspaper reporter in Australia, and he notes how he learned, 'as one always does, more from what people said to each other and took for granted in their talk, than one would have got from a hundred questions'. Here, then, in the gospels we have what the first friends of Jesus said to one another and what they took for granted.

What sort of thing did they talk about together?

A glance through some of Paul's letters – written before any of our gospels – will quickly show what they talked about. The theme of their conversations when they met together late at night in a house in the back streets of a city like Ephesus or Corinth was their new experience of God and the way their whole view of themselves and their world had been changed. What they wanted to get clear was how this new experience was to be worked out in the rough and tumble of their lives. But they would not have been talking long before the name of Jesus would come up. Indeed, it all began with him and it all centred in him. It was he who had changed their lives and given them new hope.

What, then, did they take for granted? However much they disagreed with one another about this matter or that, they all accepted that the story of Jesus was a real story of a real man. The manner of his death proved that. He had been 'crucified' – the final punishment the Romans reserved for slaves and rebels. Nobody would ever have invented that story. It would never have occurred to anybody that God's 'Chosen Leader' ('Messiah') – as they now believed Jesus to be – could die like that.

So what we have to remember when we are reading the stories about Jesus in the gospels is that they are stories with what we might call 'two levels'. They tell us a lot about the men and women who first told them; and they tell us a lot about Jesus. His real story lies behind them, and his friends told it as best they could. We have, therefore, to sort the stories out. This explains why I have arranged this book as I have done. I have used the stories about Jesus, as far as I can, as his friends told them, so that you can judge them for yourselves; and I have kept what his story means to me for a *Personal Epilogue*.

Here, then, you have the portrait of Jesus as I see him, first largely in the language of his friends, and then in my own language.

Contents

To put you in the picture

Part One: Galilean Builder

Part Two: Lord and Leader?

Acknowledgments

Anybody who sets out to write an account of Jesus must lose tally of all those who have helped him. Books he has read, conversations with students and friends, correspondence over the years make his debts quite beyond proper acknowledgment. I hope those who have helped me will not think that, while I may have sometimes disagreed, I have not learned from them more even than I myself am aware.

There are a number of my friends who from time to time have read in part or discussed in detail the material that follows in this book. I am grateful to them. But, in particular, I must thank three of my friends. Dr Graham Stanton, Professor of New Testament Studies in the University of London, King's College, has given me the benefit of his judgment over the whole manuscript, and I have been glad to accept his suggestions, without, of course, committing him in any way to what I have finally written. Dr Dennis Ellis has read it through and made important comments. Dr Francis A. D. Burns, Head of the English Department of Newman College, Birmingham, has again guided me with comments and suggestions about vocabulary and idiom. Most of all, I am deeply indebted to my wife. The heavy burden of typing is not the only burden she has carried for me; her constant encouragement and criticism – those two very necessary disciplines – have helped me more than she knows.

ALAN T. DALE

I add here, for those who might like to go further, the particular books that I have had by me in the making of this book and from which I have occasionally quoted (in brackets I give an abbreviation of each title):

C. K. Barrett	*New Testament Background: Selected Documents (NTB),*	SPCK, 1974
C. K. Barrett	*Jesus and the Gospel Tradition (JGT),*	SPCK, 1975
Martin Hengel	*Victory over Violence (VV),*	SPCK, 1975
Martin Hengel	*Crucifixion (C),*	SCM, 1977
John Hull	*Hellenistic Magic and the Synoptic Tradition (HMST),*	SCM, 1974
T. W. Manson	*The Servant Messiah (SM),*	CUP, 1953
Bo Reicke	*The New Testament Era (NTE),*	Black, 1968
Etienne Trocmé	*Jesus and his Contemporaries (JC),*	SCM, 1973
Josephus	*The Jewish War* (transl. G. A. Williamson) *(JW),*	Penguin, 1959
A. Alt	*Where Jesus Worked (WJW),*	Epworth, 1969

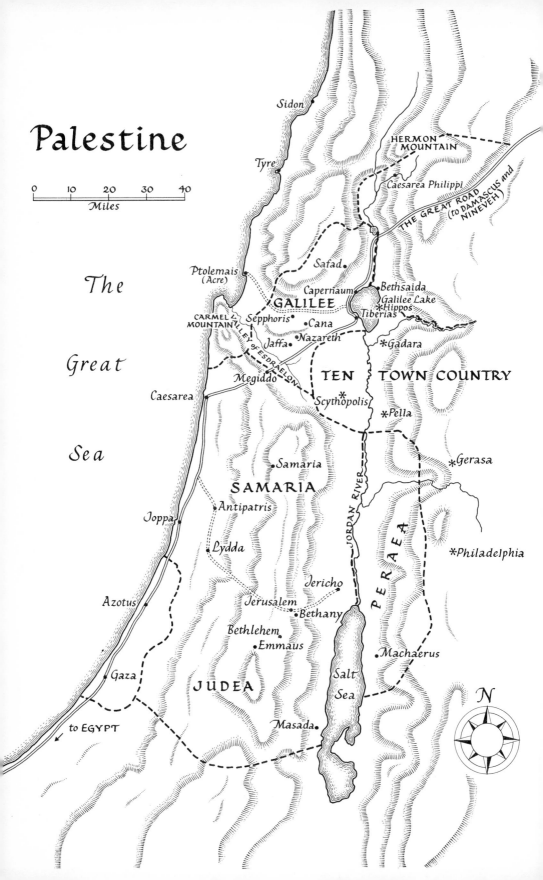

To put you in the picture

THREE SNAPSHOTS

. . . *of the country*

. . . *of the people*

. . . *of Jesus*

'Where the sycomore trees grow'

The events we are about to describe happened in Palestine nearly two thousand years ago. They ended in a southern city – the capital city, Jerusalem; but they took place mostly away in the north, in small villages and market-towns among high hills or by an inland lake.

It was quiet among the hills in the small hamlet of Nazareth where Jesus grew up. The great world of cities and empires seemed far away. By day, farmers would be out in the hot still fields; at night, the day's work done, people would be gossiping on the village threshing-floor or on the flat roofs of the houses.

The great world, however, was not really far away. The hills looked down, towards the south, over a wide and famous valley a thousand feet below; on the east, they dropped down to a busy inland sea, Lake Galilee.

Along the great valley ran a famous and important road – the Via Maris, the Sea Road. It started in Egypt in the south, and went on northward to bustling cities and celebrated countries – Damascus and Babylon, India and China. It was a very old road. For thousands of years merchants with their donkeys and camels and soldiers with their baggage could have been seen moving slowly along the valley. Great battles had been fought there.

The Lake on the east lay nearly seven hundred feet below the level of the sea – a hot, sub-tropical place. Fishing boats crowded the water. Capernaum, on the north-west shore, was a small but very lively port on the 'Sea Road', with a military post and customs station. It was the centre of a fishing industry.

The Lake was full of clear water and edged with sandy beaches. Away to the north-east, you could see Mount Hermon, nine thousand feet high, its peak touched with snow – even in summer. In the countryside around everything seemed to grow – walnuts, palms, olives, grapes, figs. There was fruit all the year round.

The hills rising above the Lake to the west were covered with woods. Olive orchards and vineyards climbed the slopes of the valleys. Sycomore trees grew everywhere.

Nazareth itself, high in a bowl of the hills and off the great roads, gave a boy time to stand and stare – to watch the storks flying north, study the bright flowers of the brief spring, and note the wild grass

> blowing in the field today –
> a bonfire on the farm tomorrow.

And what boyhood memories of looking down on the great valley lie behind these later words?

> God is your Father, and you must live in his Way. He cares for everybody everywhere – bad people and good people, honest people and dishonest people. See how the sun shines and the rain falls on all their farms alike.

'Fighters from childhood'

The villages in the Galilean hills seemed, as we have said, to be quiet sleepy places. But behind the quietness there was a very different story to tell – as we would soon have found out if we had joined in the conversation, on a Saturday morning, after worship in the synagogue or sat talking in the evening with some of the villagers. We would have quickly learned that there was trouble afoot – and dangerous trouble at that – in this northern border province.

Suppose that, one day, we climb, from the wide valley below, up the steep road to the hamlet of Nazareth. We come, after a long, stiff pull, to a gap in the skyline and find ourselves looking over into a small depression shut in by the hills rising round it.

Two men are working in the field nearby.

The village lies before us on the lower slopes of the opposite hills. We feel that the busy world has just passed it all by. A mile or two to the west, we can see the walls of the fortified town of Japha (Nazareth was probably founded from it). Behind us we can look down into the Great Valley, faint in the hot sun.

The two men come over and join us.

'It looks quiet enough here,' we say to start conversation.

'You might think so,' one of them replies, 'but it isn't – I can tell you – not by a long way!'

'It's the foreigners – they're everywhere! Look – can you see those soldiers moving along the road down there in the valley? They'll be changing the guard at Capernaum, I guess, or (pointing to the east) at the post they have on Mount Tabor over there. They think they rule the world. That's Judea across the valley – it's got a Roman governor. We've got King Herod, but he has to do what they tell him. We all have to do what they tell us.'

'They're just everywhere, these foreigners. See that hill, over there – to the south-east? There's a big foreign city beyond it, Scythopolis. Foreigners own it and the land round it. They talk Greek and they live Greek – Greek temples, Greek houses, Greek everything. There are a dozen more cities like it over on the other side of the Jordan valley. It's all wrong. It's our country, not theirs.'

'Why, foreigners own half the land round here, especially down by the Lake – large estates with landlords living miles away and managers in charge. Our land, our money! I could tell you some stories about what goes on.'

'Look over there to the west. See that glimpse of the sea and that mountain to the south of it? That's Mount Carmel. It's ours – it's where Elijah met the pagan prophets. But who owns it now? Not us – the city of Tyre!'

'This is God's land. The Temple down there in Jerusalem is God's home. We are God's people. These foreigners have no right here. One day we'll drive them all into the sea. We'll be free again – free to worship God and free to live here as his people.'

'We've had plenty of trouble up here already – and we'll have more before we've finished. Do you remember (he turns to his friend) when Judas ben Hezekiah captured Sepphoris, the town over that steep hill to the north of us? It must be over thirty years ago now. He got a small army together and stormed into the town. He ransacked the army depot – the royal depot! Every man got a weapon. But the Romans sent their troops in. A Captain Gaius came and captured the town. They burnt it to the ground – and sold the people into slavery. That's what they do.'

'Herod's rebuilt the city since then.'

'Yes, but you wouldn't know it now from one of those Greek cities I told you about.'

'Do you remember when the Romans took over the government in the south? They wanted to take a census of the people – to make them pay their new taxes. Judas (a different Judas – they call him the "Galilean") raised an uproar. He got a small army of men together and we went south to help the folk down there. We nearly stopped the census and the taxation! But it didn't get us anywhere. We weren't strong enough. But we will be one day.'

'We mean business. A lot of us in the town over there are getting ready for the real war – God's War – when God will destroy them all. God is our only Ruler and King. We'll not call any man "King" or "Governor".'

'We really mean business – that's why we call ourselves "Zealots". God's on our side; it's his law and his rule and his land we'll be fighting for – when the time comes. We've had to do it in the past, and we'll do it again. We won't be stopped this time – we'll die rather than go on living like this.'

We soon begin to understand why the very name 'Galilean' meant, to the people in the south, something like 'rebel' or 'anarchist', why Galilee was a home of the Zealots or freedom fighters, and why the Galileans were called 'born fighters'.

The war with the Romans broke out some thirty years later. The Tenth Legion marked down Japha town – and nearby Jotapata – and destroyed it in some of the bloodiest fighting of the war.

Incident in the hills

The grass was green. It was a familiar spring day, dry and hot with an east wind blowing and a yellowish haze hiding the hills and washing the colour from sea and field.

From early light the streets of the small lakeside fishing port – Capernaum – were crowded with men and loud with gossip and argument. The soldiers at the small Roman outpost in the town were wondering what was afoot.

Somebody suddenly noticed a small boat putting out.

'There he is!' he called out. 'There he is!'

The boat was making heavy weather – an on-shore wind was blowing.

The crowd – several thousand men – walking, pushing, running, made their way along the shore. The men in the boat saw what was happening; there would be no escape. They put the boat back to land.

Jesus climbed out. He knew the crowd: farmers from the hill villages, fishermen from the lakeside towns. He had grown up with some of them. They were men of the Resistance Movement – 'Zealots', nationalists – farmers or fishermen by day, 'freedom fighters' whenever the chance came.

As he looked at them he felt sorry for them, and some words from an old story came into his mind: 'like sheep without a shepherd to look after them' (you can read the story in *Winding Quest*, pp.230–231). That's what they looked like – a leaderless mob, an army without a general.

He went with them into the hills, to a lonely spot out of sight and reach of the Roman garrison.

The talk went on and on. They wanted him to be their leader – their 'king'. Jesus would have no part in their plans.

It was now late afternoon. He got everybody to share a common meal together, a meal in which they promised again to live as God's People. The men – under command – sat down in companies of fifty and a hundred each, rank by rank.

Jesus had to deal with both his friends and the men.

He got his friends to go back to the boat and across the Lake. He had to force them to go – they wanted to stay.

He then said goodbye to the men and got them to go home.

He himself, under the darkening sky, climbed the hillside. He wanted to think things out in God's presence – alone.

Part One

GALILEAN BUILDER

Jesus and his countrymen

The issue at stake

The three 'snapshots' set the scene for the story we have to tell: a turbulent northern border province, with a people who were angry that their country, capital city and temple should be at the mercy of foreign soldiers.

For thirty years at least, Jesus had lived as a builder. His village (as we have said) lay but two miles from the walled town of Japha, the government centre for the area. His work would take him away to neighbouring towns and villages. He may even, as a boy, have helped his father in the rebuilding of Sepphoris when it was destroyed by Roman soldiers. Business would take him sometimes down to the Lake and the noisy streets of Capernaum. He could not help being drawn into the heated discussions of the day.

There were almost as many points of view as men arguing about them. But all would agree that their people – the Jewish people – were a special people called by God to take a special part in the history of the world. Jesus would have no quarrel with that. But everything turned on what was meant by the words being used – by the word 'God' and by the words 'God's People'. It was not enough just to use the words, as though it was quite plain what they meant and as though everybody agreed about what they meant. It wasn't plain and they didn't agree. This was what the great debate was about. They were using the same words, but making them mean very different things.

Everybody knew, however, that things could not go on as they were. The situation in which the Jewish people found themselves – subjects of a foreign empire – was really intolerable. The only people who thought it wasn't were members of the aristocratic government in Jerusalem – they owed their very existence to their Roman overlords. The common people and their leaders – and, most of all, the best among them – longed for a great change. They felt that the root of the trouble was that they were an occupied country; if only they were free and independent, the 'good time' they all longed for would come. It was the presence of unbelieving foreigners – Roman soldiers, Greek citizens, foreign landlords – that made living as 'God's People' impossible.

Most people believed in some kind of what we would now call

'apartheid', keeping themselves 'separate', having nothing to do as far as possible with foreigners.

Lots of ordinary people, of course, simply could not avoid meeting foreigners and having to deal with them – using their money with its hated image of the emperor on it, carrying army baggage, working on foreign estates, selling market produce in Greek cities. 'Religious' people, like Pharisees and Zealots, had as little to do with foreigners as possible. They would not enter a house owned by a foreigner and they certainly would not have a meal with him. The word 'Pharisee' was believed to mean 'separatist'.

Foreigners, however, were not the only trouble. Living as 'God's People', the Pharisees and Zealots believed, meant keeping God's laws. Those 'laws' were written down long ago in the 'Torah' (the first five books of the Bible). They were kept up to date by Bible scholars. For example, God had said in the 'Torah' that his People 'must keep the Sabbath day holy' and that on it they 'must not do any work'. What did that mean in their very different situation? The Bible scholars worked out the rules of what 'working on the Sabbath' meant if God's law was to be kept in that different situation. For many people believed that it was because they had not kept God's laws that God had allowed the Romans to occupy their country.

So two things were necessary: they must have nothing to do with foreigners and they must keep God's laws. Then God would come again to rescue them.

The Zealots wanted to go much further. They believed that things could only be put right by a Holy War, the violent overthrow of the Romans. They could point to many stories in the Bible to prove it.

This was the common debate in the villages. It was the debate Jesus was drawn into over the fifteen or so years when, as boy and man, he was living and working in Nazareth and the Galilean countryside. He listened and argued. He read carefully the Bible scrolls he could find either in the small Nazareth synagogue (which would probably only have 'The Torah') or in the larger synagogues of Japha and Capernaum. He did his own thinking and he made up his own mind. He listened to both Pharisees and Zealots. Was their way really God's Way? They were good, sincere people, most of them; but were they right? He had grave doubts.

The issues had slowly become clear. When, about the age of thirty, he went down to the southern Jordan River to join John the Baptist's movement, he knew where he stood.

It was not just a matter for talk and argument. Something had to be done. Somebody had to take a stand. The leadership of the Jewish people was at stake.

Who was to lead them in this critical moment of their history?

The Pharisees? The Zealots? John? Who?

Meeting House: worship and debate

Jesus owed a lot to those among whom he grew up – to his own family and its traditions and to the good and serious people of his village.

It was from them that he first heard the story of his own people. It was not told simply as a story of what happened long ago; it was a story in which he and all the others had a part to play.

He would remember, perhaps more vividly than anything else, what happened at home each year at the Festival of Passover when the house had been cleared of everything that had yeast in it. He had to ask his father 'Why is this night different from all other nights?' His father would tell him and the rest of the family the story of how, long ago, God had rescued them from Egypt. 'Every one of us,' his father told them, 'is bound to think of himself as if *he* went out of Egypt.'

If he asked his teacher at the village school why his father did this, the teacher would tell him that it was one of God's 'laws' in the Torah and quote the command: 'You shall tell your son on that day "It is because of what God did for me on that day when I came out of Egypt".'

He owed a great debt to his village teacher. It was from him that he learned to read the Bible in its original Hebrew (his spoken language was Aramaic); as he grew older he must often have read the old scrolls and talked them over with him.

His teacher would be a Pharisee and the village Rabbi. He would hold the school after worship on Saturday morning. We don't know what he thought of Jesus. (The only story we have of Jesus as a boy shows him as a lively lad noted for the way in which he went on asking questions.) We don't know, either, who his teacher was, but perhaps he was like the teacher in this story.

A teacher heard Jesus talking and knew that he had given some fine answers; so he asked a question himself.

'Which of God's commands,' he asked, 'is more important than all the others?'

'The most important command,' said Jesus, 'is this:

> Listen, O people!
> There is one God only;
> And you must love God with everything you are –
> your heart, your soul, your mind, your body.

'There is another command almost as important:

> You must love the person next to you as much as
> you love yourself.

'No other command is more important than these two.'

'Splendid, Sir,' said the teacher. 'You're right when you say that there is one God, and one God only; and that to love God with everything we are, and to love the fellow next to us as we love ourselves, is far more important than all the Temple services.'

Jesus noted his good answer.

'You are not far from being the kind of man God wants you to be,' he said.

The village synagogue (Meeting House) was hardly the quiet place our churches and chapels are; it was more like a 'Holy Town-Hall' (as one Jewish rabbi has called it). It was school and law court and place of worship all in one.

Let us imagine it is Saturday morning (the Jewish Sabbath). We are joining in the village worship when the people meet to celebrate God's goodness and the story of his people.

The service may begin with words like these:

Blessed art thou, O Lord our God, King of the world, creator of light and darkness, maker of peace and all things.

Then everybody recites together what has been called 'the Jewish confession of faith' – a statement that sums up what Judaism is:

Hear, O Israel, the Lord our God, the Lord is One, and thou shalt love the Lord thy God with all thy heart, and with all thy soul, and with all thy might!

Then may follow prayers like these:

> Look upon our affliction and plead our cause,
> and redeem us speedily for thy name's sake.

> And to the city Jerusalem return in mercy . . .
> Blessed art thou who rebuildest Jerusalem.

The yearning for freedom – freedom to worship and to live as they believe they ought to worship and live – runs through all the service.

Here is a psalm that we may hear recited or sung:

> This is no time for peace, O God,
>   for 'silence' and 'stillness'.
> Look – your enemies are crowding in,
>   those who hate you are on the march,
> with crafty plots like conspirators,
>   against your people, your treasure –
> 'Come, let us wipe them out as a nation
>   from the memory of man!'
> They come as one man,
>   sworn enemies of yours –
> Arab tribes from the east,
>   Tyrians and Philistines from the west.
>
> Let them know that you alone
>   rule as God
>   over the whole world!

Or we may hear the villagers singing a psalm that has been written not long ago, when the Romans had taken over the country, in which the worshippers ask God to give them their own king again, a king like David:

> a king strong enough to shatter the pagan rulers,
> and to rid Jerusalem of the foreigners
> who are tramping her streets
> and destroying her.

The rabbi – or a layman – may read this story from the Old Testament:

God spoke to Abraham in a vision.

'Don't be afraid,' he said. 'I am your Shield. You will have a great future.'

'What sort of future can there be for me, O God?' said Abraham. 'I've no family; my servant Eliezer will inherit all I have.'

'He shall not be your heir,' said God. 'Your own son shall be your heir.'

He led him outside his tent.

'Look up at the sky,' he said, 'and count the stars – if you can. Your descendants shall be as many as the stars.'

Abraham trusted God; it was his trust in God that made him a truly religious man.

'I am your God,' said God. 'I brought you here to give you this country as your home.'

God made a covenant with him.

'I give this land to your descendants,' he said, 'from the Egyptian border in the south to the Euphrates River in the north, with all the tribes living there.'

And at the end of the service, the rabbi may, as he often does, send the people away with this prayer:

May the Lord God set up his reign in your days and during your years . . . and in a time near at hand.

At some time or other, Jesus would have to question publicly the ideas which worship like this set out. With his people's devotion to God and their desire to live in God's way he had no quarrel. But he had come to think about 'God's Way' very differently from the way in which they thought about it. When in a Meeting House he was to speak out plainly, there would be trouble – as this story, which Luke puts at the beginning of his account of Jesus, makes very clear. This happened, Luke tells us, in his own village of Nazareth one Saturday morning.

Jesus went along to the Service of Worship in the Meeting House, and the leader of the Meeting House asked him to read the Bible to the people. The reading was from the book of Isaiah, one of God's great men of old. He stood up, opened the book and found these words –

> God's Spirit is in my heart;
> he has called me to my great work.
> This is what I have to do –
> give the Good News to the poor;
> tell prisoners that they are prisoners no longer,
> and blind people that they can see;
> set conquered people free,
> and tell everybody:
> God's Great Day has come.

He closed the book, gave it back to the leader of the Meeting House and sat down. Everybody was staring at him.

'You have been listening to the words of the Bible,' said Jesus. 'Today what God said would happen has happened.'

Everybody spoke well of him; they were astonished and charmed by the way he talked.

'Isn't he Joseph's son?' they were asking one another.

'I know what you will say to me – "Doctor, cure yourself",' said Jesus. '"We've heard all about what you did down at Capernaum. Do it here in your own village."'

'No Man of God is liked by his own home-folk,' Jesus went on.

> 'There were many widows in our own country
> when Elijah was living.
> No rain fell for three long years and more,
> people starved in town and village;
> yet God sent him to none of our own countrymen,
> but only (says the Bible) "to a widow in a foreign city".
> There were lepers in our own country
> when Elisha was living.
> Yet God made none of our own countrymen better,
> only a foreign soldier.'

The people in the Meeting House were very angry when they heard him talk like this. They got up and took him outside the village to the edge of the cliff to throw him over it.

But Jesus walked through the village crowd and went on his way.

Freedom fighters

One of Jesus's later friends was (or had been) a member of the Resistance Movement, the freedom fighters – Simon the Zealot. Jesus must have known other Zealots. When he met the five thousand men in the 'Incident in the Hills', he would be well known to many of them.

Galilee was a home of the freedom fighters, and Japha, the mother town of Nazareth hamlet – only two miles away – was probably a Zealot town.

There were many good men among the Zealots, men who were driven by desperation to believe that violence was the only way God's People would ever win their proper freedom. There were among them, of course, as in any extreme movement, many who were no more than thugs and gangsters, hiding their bloodthirstiness behind the fine language of religion; but most were sincere men. The memory of what happened when the Romans first came in 63 B.C. was still vivid and bitter. Jesus himself may have heard the story from his grandfather who would have been a boy at the time.

It happened like this.

There had been fighting amongst the Jews themselves about who should be king. Two men tried to seize the throne (many of the common people wanted neither of them). Both appealed to the Roman general Pompey to come to their help. When he reached Jerusalem, some Jews opened the city gates to him; others barricaded themselves in the temple-fortress.

Pompey built a ramp on the north side and brought up his great siege-engines. For three months the strong temple walls stood up to the battering rams. But at last, a great tower gave way, and the legionaries poured in through the breach. The city surrendered. No fewer than twelve thousand people were reported to have died in the massacre. Pompey himself broke into the 'Holiest Room' of the Temple (where only the High Priest was allowed to go) to find out what this strange Jewish religion was all about – an act which the Jews could not forgive.

But the Zealots looked further back than the sack of Jerusalem by the Romans in 63 B.C. The Old Testament itself – their Bible – was full of stories of wars against foreigners. They were described as God's wars. This was surely enough to prove that this was God's way. Was not God called 'God of the armies of Israel'? The war against Rome was a 'Holy War'. The 'Holy Land' was not the private property of the emperor (this was what Roman taxation meant to the Jews); it was God's – he alone was king there.

The Zealots cared for social justice too. When, years after the time of our story, they actually captured Jerusalem in A.D. 66 in the war with Rome, one of the first things they did was to destroy all the legal documents there, abolishing Jewish debts to Rome, breaking up the great landed estates and setting all slaves free.

They were 'thugs' and 'murderers' in the eyes of the Roman authorities and the aristocratic Jewish government in Jerusalem; they were patriots to their own people.

But Jesus had come to believe that violence was not God's way – especially the rough violence of the Zealots. He was bound to be their critic and the critic of all those who sympathised with them. Many of his stories were aimed at them as well as at the Pharisees. When he rejected their approach to him in the 'Incident in the Hills', many of his friends abandoned him. He was never able to go back to Galilee again – except once when he had to pass through it, and travelled incognito.

It needed a brave man to be as outspoken as Jesus, if he was to be true to himself and his convictions. It took some courage to talk like this in an occupied country:

If a Roman soldier forces you to carry his baggage for a mile along the road, go two miles along the road with him.

And this took some courage too:

Jesus was in Capernaum. A detachment of Roman soldiers was stationed there.

One of the captain's slaves, a man of whom he was very fond, was dangerously ill. The captain heard that Jesus was in town, and he sent a message to him by some Jewish Leaders, who were friends of his, to ask him to come and cure his slave.

They found Jesus; they were very keen to get him to help the captain.

'He deserves help like this,' they said. 'He's a friend of all Jewish people. It was he who built our Meeting House for us.'

Jesus went along with them.

He had almost reached the house, when the captain again sent some friends to meet him.

'Sir,' he sent word, 'don't go to any more trouble. It wouldn't be fitting for you to come inside my house; that's why I didn't think it was right for me to come to meet you myself. Give the word of command, and my boy will be well. I am an army officer; there are generals over me and soldiers under me, and I know what orders are. I tell this soldier to go, and he goes; I tell that soldier to come, and he comes; I tell my slave to do this, and he does it.'

Jesus was filled with admiration for this Roman captain.

He turned to the crowd.

'Believe me,' he said, 'I haven't found a Jew who trusted me like this.'

The captain's friends went back to the house, and they found the slave fit and well.

What Jesus had to say shows how appalled he was at the suffering and evil that violence even in a good cause brings. He remembered some of the poems of the prophets in the Old Testament (poems the Zealots took little notice of) and his own poems echo their spirit and their language. Here are two:

If only today you knew how to live for peace instead of war!
    You cannot see what you are doing.

The time will come when
    your enemies will throw up a palisade round you,
    besiege and attack you on all sides,
    dash down your buildings and your people,
    leave not a wall upstanding:
all because you did not see that God had already come to you
    in love, not war.

When you see the city besieged by armies,
    be sure the last days of the city have come.

Let those inside her walls escape
    and those in the villages stay in the villages.
These are the days of punishment,
    the words of the Bible are coming true.
There will be great distress among men
    and a terrible time for this people.
They will fall at the point of the sword
    and be scattered as captives throughout the world.
Foreign soldiers will tramp the city's streets
    until the world is really God's world.

No wonder then, that on his last visit to Jerusalem, as he came round the bend of the hill on the Jericho Road and caught sight of the city walls, Jesus is reported to have burst into tears.

Facing the village

How do you talk to somebody who has made up his mind and doesn't want to listen, or who is so convinced that he is right that any other view sounds to him like downright treachery or plain disloyalty? That was Jesus's problem.

But he could not keep quiet. He must appeal, publicly and openly, to his people. He wanted to persuade them to change their minds. He could not avoid public debate and he found himself in trouble in the Meeting Houses.

Here are three stories his friends remembered.

One Saturday Jesus was speaking to the people in one of the village Meeting Houses. There was a woman there who had been ill for eighteen years; she was bent double and couldn't stand upright at all. Jesus noticed her and called her over to him.

'My dear,' he said, 'be strong again.'

He touched her with his hands, and there and then she stood straight upright. She was so happy she started to tell everybody how good God was.

The officer in charge of the Meeting House was very angry that Jesus had done this on the Holy Day.

'You've got six week-days for working in,' he kept saying to the crowd in the Meeting House. 'Come along with your troubles then, if you want to be made better. Don't come here with them on the Holy Day.'

'You're only playing at being good,' said Jesus to him. 'Doesn't every one of you untie his ox or his donkey from its stall and take it out to water it on the Holy Day? This woman is as good a Jew as you are. She's been kept bent double, remember, for eighteen years. It's like being chained up day after day. Wasn't it right that she should be set free on God's Holy Day?'

One Saturday Jesus went to a Meeting House. A man with a crippled hand was there. The Jewish Leaders watched Jesus closely to see if he would heal him, though it was a Holy Day, so that they could report him.

'Stand up for everybody to see,' said Jesus to the man.

He turned to the Jewish Leaders.

'What's the right thing to do on the Holy Day? A good thing or a bad thing?' he asked. 'Make someone better or let him die?'

They said nothing, and Jesus looked round at them in anger; he was very sad because they were so hard-hearted.

'Stretch out your hand,' he said to the man.

The man stretched out his hand and it was strong again.

The Jewish Leaders went out and met with other Leaders in the south, to see what they could do to get rid of Jesus.

Jesus went back to his own village with his friends. On Saturday, he spoke to the people in their Meeting House. Everybody listened to him with amazement.

'Where does he get it all from?' they said.

'What's this learning he's been given?'

'He does such wonderful things!'

'Isn't he the builder, Mary's son? Aren't James, Joses, Judas and Simon his brothers?'

'And aren't his sisters here with us?'

Because they knew him so well, they couldn't believe he was anybody special. They didn't want to have anything to do with him.

'You know what people say,' said Jesus. 'A man of God is always well thought of – except in his own country and among his own relatives and in his own home.'

He could do no wonderful things there. He could only put his hands on a few sick people and make them better. What surprised him was that the people of his own village didn't trust him.

There are two important things to notice in these reported incidents.

The first is that it was not the prayers (though some of them he must have found difficult to pray) nor the rabbi's sermon that made Jesus angry; it was the fact that somebody in real need was there and nobody was doing anything about it. Hard-heartedness and lack of compassion made him protest. The worship of God for him was not just a matter of prayers and sermons and psalms.

The second important thing to note comes out in the story of his visit to his own village. What surprised him was that the people of his own village didn't trust him. Their distrust made it impossible for him to help them or to speak to them about what lay deepest in his heart. *They* were surprised by the way he spoke; *he* was surprised by their blindness.

These stories make another thing clear. Neither public debate nor Meeting House sermon was the way in which he could really say what he had to say to his people.

Years later, when his friends looked back at the sort of man Jesus had been, they remembered an old poem about God's Servant that seemed to describe him precisely:

> His is no trumpet call,
>   no demagogue he
>   holding forth at street corners!
> He is too gentle to break a bruised stalk,
>   to snuff a flickering wick!
>
> But his is no flickering wick,
>   his no timid heart;
> honest and plain-spoken
>   he makes the heart of religion clear.

What, then, did Jesus do?

On the road

Let us begin with some of the stories about Jesus that his friends loved to tell.

When Jesus was out on the road again, a man ran up and knelt down in front of him.

'Good Sir,' he said, 'what must I do to take my place in God's New Kingdom?'

'You use the word "good",' said Jesus. 'Why do you use it about me? You can only use that word about God himself, for only God is really good . . . You know the Ten Commandments, don't you?'

'Sir,' he said, 'I've kept the Ten Commandments ever since I was a boy.'

Jesus looked at him and liked him very much indeed.

'There's only one thing you must do,' he said. 'You want to be really rich. Well then, sell what you've got and give it to people who haven't got anything, and come and join my company of friends.'

The man's face fell when he heard this, and he went away very sad; he was a very rich man.

'How hard it is,' Jesus said, 'for a rich man to live in God's way.'

His friends were amazed to hear him talk like this.

'You know,' Jesus went on, 'you haven't grown up yet. You think it's easy to live in God's way. But it's hard for anybody to live like that. It's easier for a camel to get through the eye of a needle than for a rich man to live in God's way.'

His friends were really amazed.

'Who then can live in God's way, if a rich man can't?' they said to one another.

Jesus looked at them.

'You forget,' he said. 'What men by themselves can't do, God can. 'Don't you remember what the Bible says about God – "I know that You can do everything"?'

Peter started talking.

'Look!' he said. 'We've given up everything to come with you!'

'And I give you a solemn promise,' said Jesus. 'Nobody has left his home, or brothers or sisters, or mother or father, or children or fields, for me and the Good News – for nothing. He won't have an easy time; he'll have to be ready to face prison and death. But here and now he will get a reward: more homes, more brothers and sisters, more mothers, more children and more fields. And in the New World that's coming, he'll have a place in God's Kingdom.'

Jesus and his friends were walking along a country road. A man joined them.

'I'll go anywhere with you,' he said to Jesus.

'Foxes have dens and wild birds can roost,' said Jesus. 'I and my friends have no home.'

'Come and join my company of friends,' said Jesus to another man.

'I have to go back to my father's funeral,' said the man. 'Let me do that first.'

'There's something more important than a funeral – even your father's funeral,' said Jesus. 'You must come and tell the Good News of God far and wide.'

'I'll come and join your company of friends, sir,' said a third man. 'But let me first of all say good-bye to my family.'

'Nobody who starts ploughing and then keeps looking back at the field behind him,' said Jesus, 'is living in God's Way.'

One Saturday, the Holy Day of the Jews, Jesus was walking through the cornfields, and his friends were picking the ears of corn as they walked along.

'Look!' said the Jewish Leaders. 'Why are you doing what's not allowed on our Holy Day?'

'You don't know your Bibles very well,' said Jesus. 'Don't you remember what King David did when he and his soldiers were starving? He went into God's House and ate the special bread that was kept there. That wasn't "allowed" either, you know; only the priests are "allowed" to eat that bread. He gave it to his soldiers too!'

'Our Holy Day,' Jesus went on, 'was made to be a help to men and women; men and women weren't made just to keep the Holy Day. What is more, they themselves can say what can and what can't be done on our Holy Day.'

Here's another story that is not found in the New Testament but is preserved in some manuscripts of Luke's gospel. It's a typical country road story.

One day Jesus saw a man out at work. It was Saturday, the Holy Day of the Jews. Nobody was supposed to do any work on the Holy Day; it was forbidden by Jewish Law.

'Sir,' said Jesus, 'if you know what you are doing, you are a very happy man. If you don't – if you just don't care what you do and when you do it – you are doing a very wrong thing, and you really are breaking the law about the Holy Day.'

All these incidents took place on country roads; they help us to see what Jesus chose to do, and the kind of man he was.

First of all, he was most at home with small groups of people with whom real conversation could take place. It is only in real conversation where questions can be asked and different points of view expressed that a man can share some of his deepest convictions.

Secondly, Jesus liked people and believed in them. He met them as an equal and they found it easy to approach him and talk with him. It was from such ordinary people, met on such informal occasions, that he chose his close friends like Peter and John.

Thirdly, Jesus knew that it was the convictions and attitudes of ordinary people that needed changing. If he could help them to see what God was really like, the whole mood and attitude of the country would change and they would then really be 'God's People', God's fellow-workers.

'When two or three people,' Jesus is reported once to have said, 'meet together as my friends, I am with them too.'

That was his way.

Going out to supper

What could Jesus do to get people really to listen, to help them really to see something of his vision of God and his world?

Meeting people on country roads was too brief and casual.

So Jesus deliberately chose the evening meal – the supper table – as the place and time when he could talk most freely. (It is not an accident that a supper table is still one of the central features of a Christian church.)

Here are two stories of Jesus at supper.

One Saturday, the Holy Day of the Jews, Jesus went to the home of a Jewish Leader to have supper with him. The Jewish Leaders themselves were only pretending to be friendly; they were really 'shadowing' him.

There was a very sick man in front of Jesus. Somebody asked a question about him.

'Tell me,' said Jesus to the Leaders there. 'Today is the Holy Day; is making a sick man better *today* right or wrong?

The Jewish Leaders said nothing.

Jesus took hold of the man, made him better and sent him home.

'Is there any one of you,' asked Jesus, 'who wouldn't pull his son out of the well he'd fallen into, even if it was the Holy Day? Why, he would do that even for his ox!'

That finished the conversation.

One day a Jewish Leader, Simon by name, asked Jesus out to supper. So they went along together to his home and sat down to supper.

Now there was a woman in the town who, in the eyes of religious people, was 'a bad lot'; the people who went to the Meeting House wouldn't have anything to do with her. She heard that Jesus was having dinner in Simon's house, and this is what she did. She got hold of a bottle of real Indian ointment. She went and stood behind the couch on which Jesus was reclining. She was crying, and her tears fell on his feet. She wiped them dry with her hair, kissing them and putting ointment on them again and again.

Simon noticed all this.

'If this man was really a Man of God,' he thought, 'he'd know who was touching him like this, and what kind of woman she was. He'd know she was a bad lot.'

Jesus was in no doubt about what Simon was thinking.

'Simon,' he said. 'I've something to say to you.'

'Go ahead,' said Simon.

Jesus turned to the woman.

'You see this woman,' he said. 'I came home with you, but you didn't give me any water to wash my feet; this woman wet my feet with her tears and dried them with her hair. You didn't greet me with a kiss; this woman has kissed my feet again and again ever since she came in. You didn't give me any perfume to put on my head; she's put ointment on my feet.

'Listen: because of her great love, all the wrong things she's done – and they are many – are forgiven. You don't show much love for me, do you? But then, you don't feel you need to be forgiven.'

Jesus turned to the woman.

'All the wrong things you've done are already forgiven,' he said.

The guests started whispering to one another.

'Who's this? He's even forgiving people's sins!'

'It's your trust in me that's saved you,' said Jesus to the woman. 'Go home and don't worry.'

John the Baptist scorned the vivid life of the villages; the desert was his home where he felt nearest to God. Jesus was not like that. Indeed, there was, in government circles, a malicious joke which made a point of the contrast between John and Jesus:

> John the Baptist is mad;
> Jesus is a glutton and a drunk –
> a friend of traitors and scoundrels.

The Meeting House was no place for getting into intimate conversations. But the evening meal was. Here people were relaxed and talked freely. Here genuine conversations could take place. Here points of view could be put and explained and discussed and argued about. And further, if you are a guest, you have a guest's privileges – you can speak your mind with greater freedom. People will not necessarily agree with you; but they are more likely to listen and you have more chance of putting what you have to say in a way that means something to them. Jesus wanted men to hear what he had to say from his own lips; he didn't want them to judge him from the wild exaggerations and distortions of village gossip. If they said 'no' to him, he wanted them to say 'no' for real reasons. To be guest at the evening meal was just the chance he wanted.

Men were curious about him, too – he had the kind of attraction that lively and original men always have. It was not only the common people who liked to listen to him. Jewish leaders – for various reasons – were impressed. Jesus himself must have been a brilliant conversationalist (as one historian has described him) – just the sort of man to invite to supper.

The great issues Jesus wanted to put before his people would soon come up for fierce discussion, in one way or another, at a supper table in an occupied country. Stories of Zealot attacks on Roman military outposts or isolated detachments of troops would soon get talked about; or what Pilate had done – like the incident when he deliberately marched troops to Jerusalem with their standards, adorned with medallions portraying the Roman emperor, at the head of the marching columns – just to insult the Jewish people who believed God forbade all images like these.

Conversations at the party would be loud and long. Jesus joined in the talk going round the table. If people wouldn't listen to speeches, they could be drawn into argument. It was probably the only way by which, in the angry and stormy times in which he was living, he would ever get a hearing.

He not only went out to supper in other people's houses; he invited them to have supper with him in his own house, too.

Here are two important stories.

One day Jesus was having a meal at home with his friends. Quite a number of tax-collectors and ordinary people had been invited. Some Jewish Leaders, who had been 'shadowing' Jesus, noticed who was there.

'Why is he eating with such people?' they asked his friends.

Jesus heard them.

'Healthy people don't need a doctor,' he said, 'but sick people do.'

Jesus was at home in Capernaum, and people came crowding to him; he and his friends had no time even to eat their meals.

News of all this came to his family. They came over to look after him; they thought he was out of his mind.

His mother and brothers came and stood outside the house, and sent somebody in to ask him to come outside. The crowd was sitting round him.

'Look!' they said to him. 'Your mother and brothers are outside asking for you.'

'Who are my real mother and brothers?' asked Jesus.

He looked at those who were sitting in a circle round him.

'Here are my real mother and brothers,' he said. 'Whoever does what God wants is my real brother and sister and mother.'

The people Jesus invited to his own house in Capernaum were people who were least likely to be invited out to supper by anybody else: people like the hated and despised tax-collectors (weren't they traitors to their own people, working for the occupying power?);

and people whom religious leaders scornfully called 'peasants' and 'sinners' (they couldn't keep all the strict rules the Pharisees insisted on). These were just the very people Jesus wanted to have supper with him; God cared for everybody, not just for a select few.

A good Jew wouldn't have anything to do with such people – they made him 'unclean'. Jesus ignored all such taboos.

He put it plainly:

Is there a farmer with a hundred sheep who won't leave them on the moors – if he has lost just one of them? Won't he go after that lost sheep until he finds it?

When he finds it, how happy he is! He puts it on his shoulders and brings it home. He calls his friends and neighbours together.

'I've found the lost sheep,' says he. 'Let's celebrate!'

Is there a woman with ten coins who won't light the lamp and sweep the room very, very carefully, and look everywhere – if she has lost just one of them? Won't she go on looking until she finds it?

When she finds it, how happy she is! She calls her friends and neighbours together.

'I've found the coin I lost,' says she. 'Let's celebrate!'

God's like that!

So he didn't mind who he had supper with!

The Challenge

WHAT JESUS HAD TO SAY

His stories

Jesus put what he had to say into stories.

He must always have loved telling stories, even as a boy. Evening meals in Nazareth must have been hilarious times, and people must often have dropped into the builder's yard for more than wood! Jesus was a born story-teller; he used the story as his chief way of making clear to his fellow-countrymen his convictions about God and his vision of God's world.

So we begin with his stories.

We mustn't imagine that Jesus made these up on the spur of the moment to illustrate something he wanted to say. His stories were not illustrations – of anything. They were the way he himself thought and reached his conclusions. What he had to say is in the story – that was the only way he could say it.

Here, for example, are two of his stories about farmers.

Look! A farmer went out sowing.

As he sowed his seed,
   some fell on the path
      and the birds came and gobbled it up.

Some fell on rocky ground
   where it had little soil;
   it grew up quickly
   because the soil was thin.
When the sun was high in the sky
   it was burned up;
   because it had no roots
      it withered away.

Some seed fell among thorn bushes
   which grew up and choked it;
      it never ripened.

Some seed fell into good soil
   and ripened and grew big.

When harvest came –
    some seeds bore up to thirty seeds,
    some up to sixty seeds,
    some up to a hundred seeds.

The farmlands of a rich farmer were bearing wonderful crops.

'What on earth shall I do?' the farmer kept thinking. 'There's no room in the old barn for these grand harvests.

'I know,' he went on. 'I'll tear down my old barns and build bigger ones, big enough to hold all my wheat and wealth. "You've wealth enough for many years. Take it easy, mate," I'll say to myself. "Have a good time. Eat and drink as much as you want."'

That night he died.

What happened to his wheat and his wealth?

Jesus didn't just see a farmer out sowing or building a barn, and, there and then, use him as a picture or illustration of what he wanted to say. A farmer was, of course, a familiar sight; but Jesus's stories about him were not just 'thrown off' in a moment. They went back, perhaps, to a day in his boyhood when, walking along a country road or looking down on fields from a rooftop, the sight of a farmer striding over his fields (or building a barn) seized his imagination, as the sight of a highland girl once seized the imagination of Wordsworth. That vision stayed in his mind over the years and haunted him, until it became the story we have – a simple but profound story not just of a farmer out in his fields or building a barn, but of God's world in the making. That is why we can live with all Jesus's stories – read them again and again and find them fresh and new every time. For Jesus was a poet, as the great prophets like Amos and Jeremiah had been before him.

Poets tell us that the beginnings of their poems and stories lie far back in the memories of their boyhood. Here are some lines from a famous twentieth-century South American poet – Pablo Neruda – and they tell us how he became aware that he was a poet and that he was thinking in pictures when he was a boy about fourteen years of age:

I don't know where
it came from, from winter or a river,
I don't know how or when,
no, they were not voices, they were not
words, not silence,

> but from the street I was summoned,
> from branches of the night,
> abruptly from the others . . .
> and suddenly I saw
> the heavens
> unfastened
> and open. . . .

(*Selected Poems*, Cape, 1970)

Perhaps Jesus felt like that.
　Here are three of his stories.

A farmer lived on a farm with his two boys.
　'Tom,' he said to the first boy, 'give me a hand on the farm today.'
　'All right, Dad,' he said.
　But he didn't go.
　The farmer said exactly the same to his second boy, Bill.
　'Not I!' said Bill.
　But later on he changed his mind, and went to give his father a hand on the farm.
　Did Tom, or Bill, do what his father wanted?

A rich man had a manager.
　One day he was visiting his estates, and this manager was charged with letting them go to rack and ruin.
　He called the manager in to see him.
　'What's this I hear about you?' he asked. 'You'd better give me an account of how you've been managing things. You can't go on as manager.'
　'What shall I do?' the manager thought. 'My master's sacking me. I'm not strong enough for farm work; it would be a disgrace to start begging . . . I know what I'll do; and then, when I'm out of a job, people will open their homes to me.'
　He sent word to the wholesale traders who hadn't paid their debts, and asked them to come and see him.
　He talked to them like this.
　'How much do you owe my master?' he asked the first trader.
　'Eight hundred gallons of oil,' he said.
　'Here's your receipt,' said the manager. 'Sit down; be quick and write four hundred gallons down.'
　'You,' said the manager to another trader, 'how much do you owe?'
　'Five hundredweight of wheat,' he said.
　'Take your receipt,' said the manager. 'Write four hundredweight down.'

God's Way is like this.

One November, after the early rains, a farmer sowed his fields with corn; and he sowed good seed.

A neighbour of his had a grudge against him. One night, when everybody was asleep, he and his men came over, and sowed weeds all over the newly sown fields; and off they went.

Nobody noticed anything. The first green shoots of corn and weed all looked alike. But when the corn began to grow tall, everybody could see what had happened – everywhere weeds were growing among the corn.

'Sir,' said the farmer's slaves, 'the seed we sowed was good seed, wasn't it? Where have all the weeds come from?'

'I think I know,' said the farmer. 'Somebody has got a grudge against me; this is his work.'

'What do you want us to do, then?' they asked. 'Go out and pull the weeds up?'

'No,' he said, 'we won't do that. We might pull up the corn as well. I'll let the fields lie, corn and weeds together. I'll deal with them at harvest time. "Get the corn into the barns," I'll tell the harvesters, "and tie up the weeds in bundles; we'll use them for the winter fires."'

These stories seem, at first hearing, to be just stories of Galilean life – the sort of thing that went on in the countryside and the people who lived there. We feel we know the two boys in the first story – we've met that sort of family incident more than once. In the Galilee of his day, bandits or bad weather could make travel very difficult. Managers of farms or estates can be idle or careless or untrustworthy. Quarrels between neighbouring farmers are not unknown in any country.

So we could look through the stories Jesus told and note the people and scenes in them, and make a most vivid picture of the Galilee he knew – its farms, its dangerous roads, the slaves on the great estates, what sowing and harvest were like. Moneylenders, travellers, bandits, thieves, farm-labourers, merchants, and gatekeepers are living people in his landscape.

Jesus drew the subjects of his stories not only from the countryside he knew so well. He sometimes used incidents from the public life of his country that were common talk in the villages – like the visit, in 4 B.C. when he was a boy, of the Jewish king Archelaus to Rome to see the emperor.

He also echoed or quoted stories and poems from the Old Testament, from the history of his people, and put them to his own original

use. In his story we usually call 'The Prodigal Son' (quite wrongly, because it is about three men, two brothers and their father) he seems to retell and remake the story of Cain and Abel and their father[1]. His story of the Good Samaritan echoes an old story of an incident in a war between North and South in the days of the Hebrew kings[2]. He could quote an old poem and turn its meaning round, as he does in the story 'Out with the Sickle' (see page 73). The last two lines Jesus quotes –

> He puts in the sickle –
> harvest time's here

come from an old poem describing a great war in which God (so the poet thought) would destroy all their enemies. Jesus makes it mean something quite different.

If the *subject* of Jesus's stories seems to be the Galilee of his day, their *theme* is God's Way, 'God's Kingdom'. Jesus often makes this quite plain by beginning with the words 'God's Way is like this. . . .' His stories don't talk directly about God's Way; they talk indirectly about it, and we have to think about them very carefully before their meaning begins to come home to us – as we have to do with any poem or story. Jesus wants us to think, not to jump to conclusions – 'to be wise like serpents'. All this puzzled his friends. We are told that once they actually asked him if he couldn't put what he had to say into plain language! What they really wanted him to do was to give them simple tidy answers which they could accept and repeat without any hard thinking. But, as Jesus knew, that's no way to understand the very mixed-up world we are living in and what God is doing. 'Look!' he says. 'Listen!' He used to quote some lines from an Old Testament poem:

> Listen, you foolish and thoughtless people:
> you've eyes, but you won't look;
> you've ears, but you won't listen.

Jesus, however, gave some hints to help people to see what the stories were about. He told them about *vineyards* and *farms* – words with special echoes for Jewish listeners. They had been used in the Old Testament to describe the Hebrew people; his listeners in Galilee would recognise them and know he was not just telling an

[1] See *Winding Quest* p. 314   [2] ibid., p. 174

interesting tale. *Harvest time* had been used by Hebrew prophets and poets for the time when God would bring the history to an end and judge the peoples of the world. *Wild birds* had been used as a reference to the foreign world beyond the borders of the Hebrew state.

The Jewish leaders soon began to realise that Jesus's stories – they had probably become the stock-in-trade of the village storytellers – were not as simple as they sounded. They began to sense that Jesus was discussing government and people and the great issues of the day, and to think of them as dangerous and subversive. Jesus must be stopped.

Last of all, Jesus did not tell his stories to answer questions but to provoke them, to stab people wide awake, to make them think again. He chose his close friends from those who came back to him to ask what he was driving at. He didn't want Yes-men – or people who didn't want to do any hard thinking.

So we must not ask too quickly 'What does this story *mean?*' (It may have many meanings, as a great painting or a good poem has.) We must live with *all* the stories, not just a few familiar ones, and let them capture our imagination as real stories. We must listen to the *whole story* as a story and not ask 'What does it illustrate?'.

We can see now why Jesus threw them into the supper-table conversations, or used them when talking to village people. He wanted them to stick in people's minds and to 'bump against' one another. He was challenging the whole way his countrymen thought about God and his 'kingdom' and about the world we live in (what really makes it tick) and about men and women (who they really are). He was trying to waken their imagination and to make them look at everything in a fresh way – and use their own eyes and ears.

But what did Jesus do when somebody came back to him and asked 'What were you getting at in that story?' That's what our next chapter is about.

His poems

Jesus was always ready to talk about the great issues his stories raised or the comments they provoked. Anybody who came back to ask questions would find him a ready listener.

But he didn't 'explain' his stories – that was not their point. (The only 'explanations' of his stories in the New Testament seem to have

been the sort of thing Christian preachers said later to 'explain' them –
they don't sound the sort of thing Jesus would have said.)

He put what the stories were 'really about' – what he was 'really
driving at' into brief poems. The poems, like his stories, sound simple,
but they are not as simple as they sound. He could, as other poets have
done, breathe fresh life into what seem at first to be commonplace and
trite phrases.

The great prophets of the Old Testament – men like Amos and
Jeremiah – had put what they had to say into poems. Jesus was only
doing what they had done.

Let us look for a moment at some Hebrew poetry and how Hebrew
poets went about making it; it will help us to understand Jesus.

Here is a typical Hebrew poem – the opening stanza of one of
Jeremiah's poems:

> If a man falls down
>   he gets up again;
> if he loses his way
>   he finds the track again.
> My people have wandered from the road –
>   why don't they find their way back?

Note what Jeremiah does. He uses very simple language. He des-
cribes very common experiences – falling down or losing the way. But
he makes them describe the religious situation of his time when the
Hebrew people had almost forgotten the vision of Moses and what
God wanted them to be; he introduces the poem with 'These are
God's words'.

Note also how he balances his 'images' or 'pictures'; 'falling down'
is paralleled by 'losing the way'. Line echoes line. This is how Jesus
made his poems. But Jesus not only made line echo line; he did something which no Hebrew poet had done before him – he made stanza
echo stanza.

Here is a Hebrew poem (a hymn) and a poem of Jesus's to compare:

> Bless God, O my soul!
>
> My God, how great you are,
>   dressed in splendour and majesty,
>   clothed with light;
> stretching out the sky like a tent,
>   laying its foundations in the Great Deep;

driving the dark storm as your chariot,
   riding on the clouds as your horses –
the winds your heralds,
   the lightnings your ministers!
You built the earth on its pillars,
   set firm for ever,
the ocean covering it like a cloak,
   drowning the mountains!
At your command the waters took flight,
   at the sound of your thunder they fled –
over the hills
   down the valleys,
     rushing to their appointed place!
You set their final frontiers,
   never again to drown the earth!

Everybody who listens to me
   and then does something about it
     is like a sensible builder.
He builds his house –
   and he builds it on rock.

Then winter comes.
   The rain pours down,
   the mountain torrents come tumbling down the hillside,
   the great winds blow
     and batter the house.
But it stands up to it all –
   underneath it is rock.

Everybody who listens to me
   but doesn't do anything about it
     is like a stupid builder.
He builds his house –
   but he builds it on earth.

Then winter comes.
   The rain pours down,
   the mountain torrents come tumbling down the hillside,
   the great winds blow
     and hurl themselves against *his* house.

Down it comes
   with a tremendous crash!

Let us now look more closely at one of his poems – the poem about the lamp. It is a poem which shows his sense of fun and his humour as well as his power of putting thoughts in very simple language:

What do you light a lamp for?

To put it out?
To put it under the bed?

Or to put it on a stand
to light the whole house
and all who live in it?

The lamp he is describing is the lamp used in a small Palestinian one-roomed house. There were no windows and you could easily stumble in the half darkness. The room itself was divided into two parts. One part, with beds, chests, cooking utensils, was raised above the rest of the floor (you had to step up on to it). The other part could be used for work – or even to house the animals! To do anything in such a house, you needed to light a lamp whatever the time of day or night. The subject of Jesus's short poem was the three ways in which an ordinary lamp might be used in such a windowless house.

There are three things you can do with a lamp – and here Jesus's sense of fun comes out.

You can just put it out – who'd do a senseless thing like that?

You can put it under the bed – that's no help to anyone!

Or you can put it on a stand to light the whole house so that people in its light can do whatever they are about.

Light doesn't tell you what to do; it simply enables you to see whatever it is that you are doing.

So much for the poem. But it was spoken, we remember, in an occupied country with a resistance movement – the country we described in earlier chapters.

Who among Jesus's countrymen were wanting to put the light out?

Who among them were not caring for the whole world but only that the light should be theirs to do with it what they wanted?

What would the words 'the whole house' suggest to people who, like Jesus's friends, had listened to his stories, heard him talk and argued with him? They would remember, too, how often, in their Bible, 'light' is a description of what God is like: 'God is my light' and 'Let us walk in God's light'.

Suddenly, this apparently simple poem is opening up deep and far-reaching questions – the questions his stories provoked and illuminated.

Here are two more of his poems:

> Who are the happy people?
>   You poor people,
>   you belong to God;
>   you who are hungry now,
>   you shall have food;
>   you who are worried now,
>   you shall laugh.
>
> Who are the unhappy people?
>   you rich people,
>   you have had your good time;
>   you who have plenty to eat now,
>   you shall be hungry;
>   you who are laughing now,
>   you shall be worried and sad.

> When you see a cloud coming up in the western sky,
>   you say at once 'There's a thunderstorm coming',
>   and the storm comes.
>
> When you see the south wind blowing,
>   you say 'It's going to be scorching hot',
>   and scorching hot it is.
>
> You know how to tell the weather;
>   why don't you know how to tell what is happening in
>   the world of men?
>   You are only playing at being good.

These poems, like Jesus's stories, must not be rushed. We must take time and ponder them; weigh them up, and begin with their imagery or picture. We must do what I think Jesus intended to be done – soak ourselves in the stories (not just one or two) and then come to his poems (again, not just one or two) and let them play on one another. For the background of the poems is the stories; and the point of the stories is put in the poems. And then we must remember that the real commentary on both story and poem is the way Jesus lived and what he did.

The simplicity of Jesus's poems and stories is their strength, for he was putting what he had to say in a way that ordinary people can hear and follow – if they will take the trouble and attend to what he says. Yet there are depths which the greatest minds find it hard to plumb. To be able to put things simply yet profoundly is one of the marks of Jesus which made a famous painter of our own time, van Gogh, say of him 'He is the greatest artist of us all'.

> Your eye is the lamp of your body.
>   If your eyesight is good,
>   you can see the whole world clearly;
>   if your eyesight is bad,
>   you can't see anything clearly;
>   if you are really blind,
>   how dark it is!

His conversations

We have seen something of the world Jesus grew up in and the kind of questions which people in Galilee were debating. Jesus could not escape being drawn into these arguments. Argument went on – perhaps no less heated – even between himself and his friends, walking along the road or talking after supper. Indeed, he seems to have chosen his close friends from those who came back to him to ask questions; and if you once start asking questions – genuine questions – you have to go on asking questions.

Jesus had no use for unthinking acceptance of the common assumptions of society, religious or otherwise. He would have agreed with Socrates – 'The unexamined life is unlivable' ('If you can't ask questions, you might as well be dead'). There were plenty of people around – as there always are – who wanted to stop questions being asked. Hence Jesus's conversations are among the most vivid memories of his friends.

WITH HIS FRIENDS

Here are two stories.

Jesus and his friends went out into the countryside near the new city which the Governor Philip had built in the highlands.

'People are talking about me,' said Jesus to his friends, as they were walking along the road. 'Who do they say I am?'

'Some say John,' they told him. 'Others say Elijah, and others say one of the great men of God.'

'But you,' said Jesus, 'who do you say I am?'

'You're God's Chosen Leader!' said Peter.

Jesus warned them not to say this to anybody.

He went on to tell them that he himself – and his friends as well – would have to go through hard times. He would be treated as an enemy of the Jewish Leaders and would have to face death; but his death would not be the end. He was quite open about it.

Peter took Jesus on one side and talked seriously to him. Jesus turned round and saw his other friends. He spoke seriously to Peter.

'Out of my sight, Tempter!' he said. 'You're not thinking of what God wants. You're talking like everybody else.'

James and John came up to Jesus one day.

'Sir,' they said, 'we're going to ask you for something and we want you to do it for us.'

'What do you want me to do for you?' asked Jesus.

'When you are a real king,' they said, 'make us the chief members of your government.'

'You don't know what you are talking about,' said Jesus. 'Can you go through what I must go through?'

'Of course we can!' they said.

'You'll go through what I must go through all right,' said Jesus. 'But I can't make anybody "a chief member of my government". God has marked out my leaders.'

The other ten friends of Jesus were angry with James and John. So Jesus called them all together.

'You know what it is like in the world outside,' he said. 'Those who think of themselves as bosses order their people about, and their great men are bullies. That isn't what you must do. You must turn it all the other way round. Whoever wants to be a great man among you must be – your servant! Whoever wants to be "Number One" must be – everybody's slave! I didn't come to have servants looking after me. I came to be a servant myself and to give myself to make everybody else free.'

Jesus's friends had great difficulty in getting out of their heads the widespread Jewish conviction that God's Chosen Leader when he came would establish some kind of national kingdom, with its king and government. They had grown up with this idea and took it for granted. The Zealots thought of God's Chosen Leader as a military ruler, establishing his power by military conquest. Many others who were not Zealots thought much like this, though some believed that God himself would defeat the Romans.

In our first story Jesus would have nothing to do with such ideas. He had not come to be that kind of person or to establish that kind of rule. There must have been some hard words spoken. Three times in Mark's account he used a very strong word meaning 'rebuke' or 'talk straight' (almost what we mean when we talk of 'ticking off') – once Peter used the word to Jesus and twice Jesus used the word to Peter. His friends must have thought Jesus's talk about suffering utterly impossible to believe – how could God's Chosen Leader suffer in any way or die at a foreigner's hands?

The other story shows that his friends had not learnt anything or in any way changed their minds. They make us feel as though they had never really listened to Jesus at all. In one story, as we have seen they actually quarrelled about who were going to be chief members of his government! In the next story two of Jesus's friends tried to steal a march on the others by getting him to promise them high office. Note what Jesus said: he turns upside down all accepted patterns of 'greatness' and what it means to be 'Number One'. He describes himself as being, of all things, a 'slave' or 'servant'. We can imagine the amazement of his friends – the word would surely call up in their minds the picture of a farm-labourer on one of the great foreign estates. That sort of a person?

WITH HIS CRITICS

Jesus quickly roused question and debate. Let us look a little more closely at what his critics had to say and the points they raised.

The question at stake was what religion really means. Is it a matter of rules and regulations? Rules and regulations (like rules of the road) help us to live in an orderly way. But are rules and regulations the heart of *religion*? Do they come first? Can we have too many of them? Can we begin to think more of them than we should? Are there not more important matters?

Here are two stories which raise the question of what religion is.

The first deals with Jewish religious rules about what is 'clean' and what is 'unclean' or 'dirty'. These words are not about what we normally think of as 'clean' and 'dirty'; they are religious words and might be translated as 'what God wants us to do' and 'what God doesn't want us to do'. They go back to rules and regulations in the Jewish lawbooks of the Old Testament. They were so important that when Mark told a story about Jesus taking no notice of them he put in a note about it. We will quote both Mark's note and story.

The Jewish people still kept some old customs.

They never ate anything without 'washing' their hands up to the wrist. If they bought anything to eat from the market, they sprinkled themselves with water. In the same way, they 'washed' cups, pots, and copper pans. This was not a proper wash, but just sprinkling; they thought that this was the sort of thing God wanted them to do. If anything had been sprinkled, they called it 'clean'; if it had not been sprinkled, they called it 'dirty'.

The Jewish Leaders noticed that the friends of Jesus ate their food with 'dirty' hands, and they came to talk to him about it.

'Why don't these friends of yours keep the old customs?' they asked. 'Why do they eat food with "dirty" hands?'

'You're just playing at being good,' said Jesus. 'The old words of the Bible might have been written about you –

> These people talk, talk, talk!
> They don't really love Me.
> What they do to "please" Me
> doesn't mean anything;
> what they say "God wants"
> they have made up for themselves.

'You make people do what you want them to do,' said Jesus, 'not what God wants them to do. Here's another example. God said: "Respect your father and mother"; you say: "If a man says to his parents, 'I know I ought to give this to you, but I'm going to give it to the Temple', he needn't do anything for his father or mother." So your "old custom" takes the place of God's command. I could give you many other examples.'

Jesus's answer needs little comment.

The word Jesus used here for 'playing at being good' was 'hypocrite'. This word did not mean what we now use it to mean – someone who deliberately pretends to be good. It meant, then, being inconsistent rather than insincere – the hypocrite was deceiving himself, whether he knew it or not. It is plain that Jesus thought of real religion as something much more than keeping rules, however good the rules might be. Indeed, he suggests that a man can keep all the rules and yet be very irreligious. (See the story of Jesus at supper on p.26; this is the point Paul takes up and discusses in his letter to the Christians in Rome, *New World*, pp.257ff – 301ff in 1st edn.).

The second story happened in Jerusalem towards the end of Jesus's life. In the Temple were several open courts. One of them was the Foreigners' Court where sympathetic foreigners could share in Jewish worship. It was being used in Jesus's time as a market and a bank and a short cut through the Temple – anything but a place of worship for foreigners. It looked as if nobody bothered whether foreigners worshipped there or not. Jesus cleared the courts. His very indignation took the stall-keepers and bankers by surprise; foreigners, Jesus was saying, had a place in God's worship.

The Jewish Leaders met him afterwards when he came back to the Temple. The story continues like this:

As he was walking about the Temple, Jewish Leaders came up to him.

'Who told you to do this sort of thing?' they asked. 'Who gave you the right to act like this?'

'I'll ask you a question first,' said Jesus. 'You answer my question and I'll answer yours. You remember John the Baptist; was he God's messenger, or just another of these mob-leaders? You tell me.'

They didn't know what to say.

'If we say, "He was God's messenger,"' they said to one another, 'he'll say, "Why didn't you join him, then?" If we say, "Oh, just one of these mob-leaders . . .".'

They hardly dared finish the sentence. They were frightened of the crowd, for everybody thought that John was one of God's messengers.

'We don't know,' they said at last.

'Well, I'm not telling you, then, who gave me power to do what I'm doing,' said Jesus. 'But I'll tell you a story.

'Once upon a time a man cleared the ground and made a farm. He let it out to farmers and went off abroad. At harvest-time he sent a slave for his share of the harvest, but the farmers beat the slave and sent him off with empty hands. He sent another slave, but the farmers hit him on the head and insulted him.

'The landowner had an only son; he sent him to the farm.

'"They will respect my son," he said.

'When the farmers saw him, they said to one another: "This is the son himself. Come on, let's kill him and the farm will be ours!"

'They got hold of him, killed him, and threw his body outside the farm.

'What will the landowner do? He will come himself, of course, and destroy those farmers and give the farm to others.'

The Jewish Leaders now made up their minds to get hold of Jesus, for they knew that the story was aimed at them. But they were frightened of the crowd; so they left Jesus and went away.

We can see how Jesus dealt with critics. He sometimes met a question with another question. He tried to make people do their own thinking or to force them, as here, to come out into the open. He sometimes suspected that the question he was being asked (as in this story) was not really a genuine question; he didn't intend to be caught as simply as that.

On this occasion he took up a story which Isaiah, one of the great prophets, had once told his people about a farm where only wild grapes would grow, but which he had made into his own story. The

Jewish Leaders would recognize immediately what he was doing and also see that the farm was a picture of the Jewish people and that he was criticising themselves. The farmers in the story had wanted to take over the farm and exploit it for themselves; the Jewish Leaders were now making the Temple *their* temple, not God's. They weren't asking what God really wanted them to do. No wonder that, then and there, they made up their minds that they weren't having any more radical talk like this. They decided to get rid of Jesus somehow.

It wasn't only that they disagreed with him. They were frightened lest the common people took him seriously. If they did, the whole Jewish way of life and Jewish national hopes, as the Leaders understood them, would vanish – or be changed into something they could hardly recognise. They saw more clearly than Jesus's own friends what his intentions were.

Here is another story. The Zealots and the Jewish Leaders were not the only ones who were puzzled by Jesus. John the Baptist – a good but narrow, old-fashioned sort of man – was also puzzled. He wasn't sure about Jesus. Anyhow, what *he* thought religion was about and what Jesus thought it was about were two very different things. People couldn't help noticing the difference. Some people once raised the question:

During the Fast Days, the friends of John the Baptist were fasting. Some people came to Jesus.

'Why do John's friends fast,' they asked, 'but your friends don't?'

'Can guests at a wedding leave the wedding breakfast uneaten?' asked Jesus. 'What would the bridegroom think?'

A wedding breakfast! Going out to supper! Having an evening meal together! What *did* Jesus think religion was about?

His sayings

Many sayings of Jesus were also remembered and repeated.

Most of them give no hint of when or where Jesus said them. The original occasion had been quite forgotten. All Mark and Matthew and Luke could do with them, when they came to write their accounts of Jesus, was to put them in where they seemed to fit best. Matthew arranged most of them in five groups (the 'Sermon on the Mount' is the most famous of his arrangements). Luke had come almost to the end of his account and still had many sayings and stories to record; he used Jesus's last journey to Jerusalem as the most convenient way of getting them into his story.

Sometimes, however, his friends remembered the occasion of some of Jesus's sayings, and give a brief account of where he was or to whom he was talking. Here are two such stories:

One day a crowd of people were listening to Jesus.

'Sir,' said a man in the crowd, 'when my father died my brother took all he left and kept it. Tell him to share it with me.'

'My friend,' said Jesus, 'this is not a law-court and I'm not a judge. It's not my work to settle questions like this.'

He turned to the crowd.

'Don't get greedy,' he said. 'Being a millionaire isn't the sort of thing that makes life worth living.'

Peter came to Jesus one day.

'Sir,' he said, 'how often can somebody treat me badly, and I forgive him and be friends with him again? Will seven times be enough'?

'This isn't something you can add up like sums,' said Jesus. 'The answer is – every time.'

Here are other remembered sayings:

He who is not my friend is my enemy; he who does not help me to get people everywhere to live together as God's Family, sets people against one another.

He who is not our enemy is our friend.

If you are always thinking of saving your skins, that's just what you won't do. But, if you forget all about yourself because you are keen on helping me, even if you lose your life, you will be all right. You will really be yourself.

You are my friends, and this is what I want to say to you: you must never worship men – not even men like the Roman Emperor; the worst they can do is to take your life away from you. You must worship God alone – both life and death are in *his* hands.

Why don't you make up your own minds about what is right and what is wrong?

It is a good thing to be healthy. But we may have to risk the loss of an eye or a hand sometimes; God's Way must always come first.

Don't forget this: some of those at the bottom of the class will find themselves at the top of the class; and some of those at the top will find themselves at the bottom.

When you have a party, don't always invite friends, cousins, relatives, and well-to-do neighbours; they will invite you back to *their* party, and all of you will be just having a good time together. When you have a party, give it freely; invite poor people, cripples, lame people, blind people; they can't invite you back. That's the way you'll find happiness. That's what heaven is like.

Giving makes us really happy, not getting.

If only you understood the Bible when you read it! There God says:

> It is your affection I delight in,
> not your Temple services.

If you had understood that saying, you wouldn't have got things all mixed up, and called innocent people wicked.

What it was all about: God's way

No better words than 'Good News' can describe what Jesus had to say.

It wasn't good news for everybody, of course. It wasn't good news for people who lived only for themselves and what they could get, or who thought more of their own nation than they did of the world beyond their frontiers, or who didn't bother about God at all or thought they knew all the answers. For what Jesus had to say was an attack on many of the common assumptions and traditional ways of his own people – and of people everywhere.

The first step, he insisted, if we are to have a real world, God's world, is a great change in the way we think and live. Mark summarised what he stood for in these words:

Jesus came into Galilee telling everybody the Good News about God. This is what he said:

> The Great Day is here.
> God's kingdom has come;
> change your ways
> and trust in the Good News.

The first thing to note is that Jesus did not talk about himself, as many religious leaders have done. The theme of his stories and poems and the passion of his life was, not himself, but God and his Way.

He stood for three things: God is king – the world is his world and he is in charge of it; he is Father – he cares for everybody everywhere; and Now is the important moment.

Jesus shared the conviction of his countrymen that God was king, but he did not believe that God's rule ('The kingdom of God') was what the Zealots or the Pharisees thought it was. He shared their conviction that God was Father, but this, for Jesus, was the most important personal thing to say about him and it made all the difference to what the words 'God is king' meant.

Jesus did not share his countrymen's conviction that God was somehow far off and had to be begged to come to men's help. God was here in their midst and at work among them already; he was present always and everywhere and with everybody.

All this is made very clear when we remember how Jesus prayed. When he prayed, his friends noted he did not begin his prayers in the customary Jewish way. He began with the word 'Abba' – a most unexpected way of talking to God. For 'Abba' is a family word – the way a father is addressed by his children or by his grown-up sons and daughters in the family circle. Jesus himself would have used it as a boy when addressing his own father. God was as real and close to him as that. 'Abba' would sound in Jewish ears much as 'Dad' would sound in ours. Nobody would ever use it when praying to God. Jesus did.

But Jesus did not use it in public. He did not talk about God in this way, either with his friends or anybody else. He used it only in his private prayers. But it coloured all he had to say.

This is how he put it in one of his most important poems and one of his most important stories:

> Don't worry about what you are going to eat
> > or what sort of clothes you are going to wear;
> what you are is more important than what you eat,
> > what you are is more important than what you wear.

> Look at the wild birds:
> > they don't go out farming;
> > they have no store or barn;
> God feeds them.
> > How much more than wild birds you mean to God!

Look at the wild flowers:
> they don't work like mothers at home.
Yet, believe me, King Solomon wasn't robed
> as gloriously as a wild flower.

God dresses the wild grass –
> blowing in the field today,
> a bonfire on the farm tomorrow.

How much more will God look after you!
> You don't trust him enough.

A man and his two sons were farmers.

The younger son came one day to his father.

'Dad,' he said, 'it's time you handed over the farm to the two of us. Give me my share.'

That's what the father did. He divided up the farm between his two sons, and handed it over.

The younger son quickly packed his things and went abroad. There he threw his money away having 'a good time'.

At last, his pockets were empty. Then the harvest failed all over the land. There he was – no money and no food. He took a job with a farmer there, and the farmer sent him off to feed the pigs in the fields. He felt like swallowing the pigs' food himself. Nobody lifted a hand to help him.

Then he knew what a fool he'd been.

'How many of the labourers on my father's farm have more food than they want,' he thought, 'and here I am starving to death! I'm going home to my father. I've wronged God, and I've wronged my father. I'll tell him so. And I'll tell him, too, that I don't deserve to be called a son of his; he can take me on as a labourer.'

He got up and went home.

When he was still quite a long way from his father's farm, his father saw him coming. He felt very sorry for him; and he ran out to meet him, threw his arms round his neck and kissed him.

'Dad,' the boy began to say, 'I've wronged God and I've wronged you. I don't deserve to be called a son of yours . . .'

'Quick!' his father called to the servants, 'go and get his best clothes out. Get a ring and sandals and dress him properly. And kill the calf we've fattened. We'll have a feast and a grand time tonight. My boy was dead and lost; and here he is alive and back home again!'

And they began to celebrate.

Now the older son had been out on the farm. He was coming home and had almost reached the house when he heard the sound of bagpipes and dancing. He called one of the farmhands out, and asked him what was going on.

'Your brother's back,' said the man. 'Your father's killed the calf because he's safe home again.'

The older son was furious, and he wouldn't even go inside the house. His father came out and begged him to come inside.

'Look,' he answered back, 'I've slaved for you all these years. I did everything you told me to do. But what do I get? Not even a kid to have a good time with my friends. This son of yours can throw his money away on girls, if he likes, and come home again – and you go and kill the calf for him!'

'My dear boy,' said his father. 'We're always together. All the farm is yours – you know that. We had to celebrate tonight. It's your *brother* who was dead and lost; it's your *brother* who's alive and back home again!'

Here, in this poem and story, is the heart of what Jesus had to say. What he cared for is clearly seen if we put them alongside, in contrast, the lines from the psalm we quoted on page 15 or some words from the rules of the Qumran monastery down in the Jordan Valley near the Dead Sea. The last lines of the psalm ran:

> May the Lord hasten his mercy upon Israel!
> May he deliver us from the uncleanness of unholy enemies!
> The Lord is our king for ever and ever.

The rules of the monastery contained these words:

No madman, or lunatic, or simpleton, or fool, no blind man, or maimed, or lame, or deaf man, and no minor shall enter the Community. . . .

For Jesus, these were the very people God cared for.

The story and the poem show, too, how God is still at work in his world, still bringing it to be the kind of world which is a real family and in which nobody at all is left out.

If these great convictions have any truth in them, the world is not an evil place, it is God's world – a world where evil can be beaten by good. Men and women are born in God's image, and are free to choose. They are free to choose evil – and they are free to change their minds. They can be sorry for the wrong things they have done, and they can be forgiven. And in all this, they have God their Father's help.

That is why Now is important. There is a strong sense of urgency in the way Jesus spoke. He believed that he and the whole world stood at a turning point in history – that, indeed, the end of the world as we know it was near when God would bring in a new age.

The Jews had for some time been talking about *two ages*: the present age which is evil and corrupt; and the 'age to come' or 'new age', when the present evil age will have disappeared, and 'the new age' ruled over by God would appear. Jesus shared this way of talking but changed its meaning.

This sense of urgency did not spring just from his belief that the existing order of things was near its end. It sprang from his sense of God's presence among men. If God is present in human history, if he is making his world and if he can be addressed as 'Abba', every moment is of vast consequence and its possibilities, in God's love, are undreamed of:

Trust in God – even though it is as small as a mustard seed – can move mountains or pull up a mulberry bush with its long roots.

The urgency of Jesus is heard in these stories and sayings:

God's Way is like this.
    A man left home and went abroad. He put his slaves in charge of everything; each has his own job.
    'Keep a sharp look out,' he said to the gatekeeper.

'When shall we really see people living in God's Way?' a Jewish Leader once asked Jesus.
    'This isn't the sort of thing that happens all of a sudden,' said Jesus. 'You can't *see* it. Nobody will say, "Ah! Here it is!" or "There it is!" It's here now.'

A man was going down the road from Jerusalem to Jericho, and fell into the hands of bandits. They tore off his clothes and beat him up. Then off they went, and left him lying half-dead on the road.

Quite by accident, a priest was going down the same road. He saw the man lying there, but he didn't stop. He went on past him – on the other side of the road. It was just the same with a Temple caretaker. He, too, came to the spot and saw the may lying there; he, too, didn't stop – he went on past him on the other side of the road.

Then a foreigner, who was on a journey across the country, came upon the man. He saw him lying there, and felt very sorry for him. He went across to him, put ointment on his wounds and bandaged them up. He lifted him up on to the horse he had been riding, and brought him to an inn and looked after him.

Next morning, he took a pound out of his purse and gave it to the inn-keeper.

'Look after him,' he said. 'If it costs more than a pound, I'll put it right with you on my way back.'

'Keep awake!' 'Be ready!' 'Keep on the alert!' Every moment is an urgent one – whether in Jesus's century or our own.

Was Jesus just guessing? How was he so sure?

He may have been mistaken, but he was not guessing.

Three things are clear:

First, he looked the actual world he lived in, as he saw it in the lively border province of Galilee, straight in the face. He knew what kind of world it was and the sort of things men were capable of. He had no illusions. He was down-to-earth and realistic. It was the others who were dreaming and could not see what was really happening.

Secondly, he drew on the strength of his own experience of God which, as we have seen, was summed up in the way he addressed God in his prayers: Abba ('Dad'). Whatever happened, however dark the world seemed to be, he held on to this sense of God's presence. It was the guiding light by which he found his way.

And finally, he had the whole story of his people to guide him – what those before him had discovered about God. The prophets had, as their clue, the story of how God delivered a handful of tribesmen – the lowest of the low – from Egyptian slavery. Moses saw that if God had delivered them like this it must be because he was a God who cared, not a remote God who took no notice; and if he was a God who cared, then he must care for everybody everywhere – there are no geographical boundaries to love. Prophets like Amos and Jeremiah worked out this insight and showed how it changed people's whole view of the world. For Jesus too, his people's story was a clue to making sense of what God was doing.

Here is one of his prayers:

> I praise You, Father,
>   Lord of the world –
> very clever people have missed the secret of your heart,
>   simple people have found it.
>
> Yes, Father, I give glory to you;
>   this is your way.

The best guide, however, to what Jesus was 'driving at', what really mattered to him, was the way he lived. We turn now to see what he did.

WHAT JESUS DID

A day in his life

Near the beginning of his account of Jesus, Mark described a day in his life – what happened from about 10 o'clock one day to dawn the next day. He used it as a brief sketch of the man whose story he was going to tell. It reads as if it went back to eye-witnesses, as it may very well have done (it may even have come from Peter himself).

Jesus and his friends were in Capernaum, a fishing town on the shores of the Lake. It was Saturday, and Jesus and his friends went along to the Meeting House and took part in the Service of Worship. There was a madman among the people who had gathered there.

'What are you bothering us for, Jesus, coming here from Nazareth?' he shouted out. 'Have you come to get rid of us? I know you – you're God's Holy One!'

'Be quiet,' said Jesus severely, 'and come out of him.'

The mad spirit in the man threw him on the ground, and, shouting out loudly, came out of him. Everybody was taken by surprise, and started talking about Jesus and what he had said and done:

'What's this?'

'It's not like anything we've heard before!'

'He talks to mad spirits as though he was their master!'

'And they do what he tells them!'

Jesus and his friends left the building and went along with James and John to the home of Peter and Andrew. Peter's mother-in-law was in bed with fever. They told Jesus about her. He went to her and took hold of her hand and lifted her up. The fever left her and she looked after the visitors.

At sunset, when the Holy Day was over, people brought all who were ill to Jesus. The whole town crowded round the door of the house. Jesus made them all better, whatever their illness was.

Early next morning, while it was still dark, Jesus got up and went out of the house to a lonely place. Peter and his friends hunted him out and found him – praying.

'Everybody's looking for you,' they told him.

'Let's get away,' said Jesus, 'and give them the Good News in the nearby market-towns. That's why I came out here.'

We must keep this story in mind as we go on to look at the different kinds of stories people told about Jesus.

We will begin with the popular stories that were being told about him in the villages, and then go on to listen to stories his friends told one another and used in their preaching in Palestine and throughout the Roman world.

Talk in the market

Jesus was one of the most talked-about men in Galilee. Everybody had heard about him. There had been notorious Galileans before him – people like Judas 'the Galilean' we have already met. Jesus was, perhaps, the most famous Galilean of them all.

He was a striking figure. The gossip of the bazaar and the village nearly always exaggerates and distorts reports, and stories always grow in the telling. But they often enough seize on important aspects of the person they are about; people don't make up these stories from nothing. There is something in the picture they paint we need to take seriously.

Here are two stories about Jesus which probably go back to the villagers of Galilee; we might have heard them told if we had stopped to listen to a story-teller at a fair or overheard people talking on a village threshing-floor. The story-teller was the means by which news spread from village to village.

It was getting dark.

'Let's go across the Lake,' he said to his friends.

They left the crowd and took him along with them in the boat just as he

was. Other boats, too, put out to sea with them. Suddenly a wind blew up.
The waves were breaking into the boat and filling it with water. Jesus was
sleeping on a cushion in the stern.

They woke him up.

'Sir,' they shouted, 'doesn't it matter to you that we're sinking?'

Jesus woke up.

'Silence!' he said to the wind and the sea. 'Be quiet!'

The wind dropped and there was a dead calm.

'Why are you cowards like this?' he said to his friends. 'Don't you trust
God yet?'

They had been very frightened indeed.

'What sort of man is this?' they asked one another. 'He's master even of
wind and sea!'

One day Jesus and his friends sailed to the far shore of Galilee Lake.

A madman lived among the graves there. Nobody had been able to tie him
up even with chains. He had often been tied up with handcuffs and chains,
but he had torn the handcuffs apart and smashed the chains. Night and day he
lived among the graves and on the hills, shouting out and striking himself
with stones. Nobody could tame him.

Jesus got out of the boat. The madman saw him from a long way off, ran
to him and knelt down at his feet.

'What are you bothering me for, Jesus, Son of the Most High God?' he
screamed at the top of his voice. 'I beg you, in God's name, don't torment
me!' For Jesus was already saying to him – 'Come out of the man, you foul
spirit.'

'What's your name?' asked Jesus.

'I'm the Roman Army,' he said. 'There are thousands of us.'

He begged Jesus over and over again not to send the foul spirits away from
the graves and the hills. A great herd of pigs was feeding on the hillside.

'Send us into the pigs,' said the spirits. 'Let us get inside them.'

Jesus let them go, and the foul spirits went off into the pigs. The herd
rushed down the steep bank into the sea – all two thousand of them – and
were drowned.

The herdsmen ran off and told the news in town and country; everybody
came out to see what had happened. They came to Jesus and looked at the
madman now sitting down, wearing his clothes and quite sane, the very man
who had called himself 'The Roman Army'. They were frightened. Those
who had seen what had happened told the others about the madman and
about the pigs; and they all begged Jesus to go away. They didn't want him
there.

As Jesus was getting into the boat, the man himself begged to join his
company of friends; but Jesus wouldn't let him join them.

'Go home to your own people,' he said, 'and tell them what God has done for you and how he has had pity on you.'

Off he went, and everywhere in 'Ten Town Country' he told people what Jesus had done to him. It amazed everybody.

We can see what struck people about Jesus. He had what can only be described as authority and power.

There was something commanding about him that made people speak of him as a magician, able to still a storm or walk on water. (There were plenty of stories going the round of the villages about magicians and their exploits and of rabbis as magicians.) Many of their stories, however, were about his 'power' to heal people – as he healed the madman who made a Roman military cemetery his home and thought the spirits of the dead legionaries were his masters.

They talked about Jesus as a famous exorcist (a man who can expel evil spirits); they remembered for a long time how he could cure demon-possessed people.

How these popular stories came to be remembered and written down we do not know; perhaps Mark was the first to use them.

Friends' stories

Most of the stories we have about Jesus come from his friends.

Here are three typical stories: about a Jericho beggar, the manager of the Tax Office in the same town and a cripple and his companions.

Jesus and his friends were leaving Jericho by the Jerusalem Road. There was a large crowd with them. A blind beggar, Bartimaeus, was sitting at the roadside; he heard people saying, 'It's Jesus from Nazareth.'

'Son of David! Jesus!' he shouted. 'Have pity on me!'

The crowd told him to be quiet, but he went on shouting 'Son of David! Have pity on me!'

Jesus stood still.

'Call him over here,' he said.

Everybody then started calling the blind man: 'Cheer up!' 'Get up!' 'He's calling you!'

The beggar threw his cloak off, jumped up and came to Jesus.

'What do you want me to do for you?' asked Jesus.

'Sir,' he said, 'give me my sight back again.'

'Go home,' said Jesus. 'It's your trust in me that has made you better.'

His sight came back, and he followed Jesus along the road.

One day Jesus was going through Jericho City.

Now there lived in Jericho a very rich man called Zacchaeus, manager of the Tax office there. He was very keen to see what sort of person Jesus was; but he was a little man and he couldn't see over the heads of the crowds. So he ran on ahead along the road Jesus was taking, and climbed into a fig tree to get a good view of him.

Jesus came along the road and looked up at Zacchaeus in the tree.

'Zacchaeus,' he said, 'you'd better be quick and get down – I must stay with you today.'

He was down in a moment, thrilled to have Jesus as his guest.

The crowd didn't like it.

'He's staying with that scoundrel of a fellow,' they muttered.

Zacchaeus stopped.

'I'm not the man they think I am, Sir,' he said to Jesus. 'Look, I give half my income to people in need; and if I've taken more than I ought from anybody, I give four times as much back.'

'God himself has come to this home today,' said Jesus. 'This man belongs to God's family too. You know what God said in the Bible – "I will seek the lost". That's what I and my friends are doing.'

One day some men brought a cripple to Jesus. Four of them were carrying him. The crowd was so great that they could not get anywhere near him. So they stripped the flat roof off the house where Jesus was, dug a hole and lowered the mat with the cripple on it.

Jesus saw how these men trusted him.

'I'm speaking to you,' he said to the cripple. 'Get up, pick up your mat and go home.'

The cripple got up, picked up his mat and walked out.

Everyone kept looking at him in amazement and thanked God for his goodness.

'We've never seen anything like this!' they said.

These stories speak for themselves. They show how Jesus captured the imagination of common people. Here is his utter disregard for himself, his reputation or his safety, and his deep concern for others. He never asked who they were; their need was the only thing that mattered.

It was not just that he was a kind man. He was certainly kind, but his love of men and women went much deeper. It sprang from his convictions about God: God cared for everybody; he too, therefore, must care for everybody.

It was in his caring for people – whoever they were, whatever their need – that Jesus made God's care real. Nobody, for him, was left out of God's family or out of the range of his care.

The making of a real world

One of the most striking things about Jesus was the way he thought about the world we live in. It was certainly a rough and dangerous world. Evil often seemed to be master. Yet, Jesus believed with all his heart that it was God's world – his Father's world.

The striking thing is this: Jesus believed that God was still making his world. It wasn't something he had made a long time ago and then left to itself. He was not an absentee God; he was working still. 'God is at work,' Jesus was reported to have said, 'and so I'm also at work.'

Here is how he himself once put it – a story and a saying:

God's Way is like this.

It was harvest time, and a farmer went out to the market square to hire workmen for his vineyard. He settled with them for the proper wage for the day – a pound – and sent them out to work.

About nine o'clock he went out again. Men were hanging about the square with nothing to do.

'You, too, can go and work in the vineyard,' he said, 'and I'll pay you the proper wage.'

Off they went to work.

At noon and at three o'clock in the afternoon he went out to the market square again, and the same thing happened.

About five o'clock he went out again to the square. Men were still hanging about.

'Why are you hanging about all day doing nothing?' he asked.

'Nobody has taken us on,' they said.

'You can go into the vineyard with the others,' he told them.

By now it was evening. The farmer spoke to his foreman.

'Call the workmen in,' he said, 'and pay them their wages. And start with the last ones we took on.'

Those who started work at five o'clock in the afternoon came up and got a full day's wage – a pound.

Then those who had started work at six o'clock in the morning came up they expected to get more than that. They, too, got a full day's wage – a pound.

They began to go for the farmer.

'These fellows who started last have only done an hour's work!'

'And you are treating them like us!'

'We've had to do all the hard work!'

'And we've had the scorching sun to put up with as well!'

The farmer tackled their leader.

'My dear man,' he said, 'I'm not treating you badly. Didn't you settle with me for a proper day's wage? Take your money and get out. I'm going to give these fellows who started at five o'clock the same wage I'm giving you. Can't I use my own money as I want to? Does my generosity make you jealous?'

God is your Father, and you must live in his Way. He cares for everybody everywhere – bad people and good people, honest people and dishonest people. See how the sun shines and the rain falls on all their farms alike.

The whole style of Jesus makes it clear that for him the world – what we should now call our 'universe' – is a living world. It is neither meaningless nor haphazard. It is not fixed so that nothing can really happen because everything is already rigidly determined. It is his Father's world, full of untold possibilities and promise. It is God's Family in the making.

That is why Mark can tell us that the whole theme of what Jesus stood for can be described in the words –

> The Great Day is here,
> God's kingdom has come.

The idea of a 'Great Day' ('God's Day') goes back a long way in the history of the Jewish people. It once stood for the day of victory when they had defeated their enemies with (as they believed) God's help. Then the prophets thought of it as the day when God would triumph over all that is evil. This is how Jesus thought of it. But he also believed that God's Day was now at hand and a new world that would really be God's world was being born. It was his work to announce it and be God's fellow-worker in bringing it in.

Here are his own words:

> The time is coming when you will long to see God's new world
>   and you will not see it.
> 'Here it is!' somebody will say, or 'There it is!'
>   Don't run after them.

> For as the lightning lights up the whole sky
>   God himself will light up the whole world.

> What happy people you are
>   to see what you are seeing!
> I tell you this:
>   Kings and great men of old longed to see what you are seeing,
>   but did not see it;
>   they longed to hear what you are hearing,
>   but did not hear it.

The Old Testament prophets thought of God's Day as a dark day because there was so much evil in the world and so many people did not want to live in God's Way. Jesus thought of it as the Day when God's love would triumph.

Nobody has understood Jesus better than Paul. Jesus had changed the whole way he thought – 'We look at everything differently now'.

The world, we now know, is not a meaningless world. God has had a purpose from the beginning. He created the world so that men and women everywhere should learn to live gloriously as members of his Family.

This is God's 'secret' and his 'wisdom'.

The governments of the world didn't realise what God was doing; if they had known anything about it, they wouldn't have executed Jesus as a criminal – Jesus who showed us, in the way he lived, what God was really like.

An old poem puts it clearly:

> 'Human eyes have never seen,
> human ears have never heard,
> human minds have never thought
> what God keeps ready
> for those who love him'.

How then did Jesus think God's fellow-workers ought to live? He himself showed us what it meant to 'love God with all we are and to love our neighbour – the man or woman next to us, whoever they may be – as ourselves'. And he gave us what we might describe as his 'Rule for God's fellow-workers' in what we know as 'The Lord's Prayer'. The original short poem ran something like this:

> Father
>> may your name be used with reverence,
>> may everybody live in your way.
>>> Give us today our bread for tomorrow.
>> Forgive us as we forgive others;
>> do not put us to the test.

When this poem became the public family prayer of Christians, 'Father' ('Abba' – see p.57) was changed to 'Our Father in heaven' and a sentence of praise was added to it:

> Yours is the kingdom and the power and the glory
> for ever, Amen.

Note where we must begin: we must remember what God himself is like – Abba, Father; this must govern all we say and think and do. Then we must go on to remember, not our own needs, but what God is doing – his name, his will, his kingdom – his 'Way'; for, if we are to be his fellow-workers, we must know what he is doing. 'You must make God's Way your aim,' Jesus once said, 'and God will give you all the other things as well.' It can never be the other way round.

Our health must come next – we must be as fit as we can be.

Our own needs come last – for forgiveness and God's care.

Can a real family world be made in any other way?

What did Jesus do about it?

WHAT JESUS PLANNED

The job he inherited

Jesus believed that God had called him to the leadership of his people. But he came to think of 'leadership' in a very different way from that in which either the freedom fighters or the religious authorities thought of 'leadership'.

We all grow up with some idea of our own national history, its events and its outstanding people. No country in the world has so remembered its past and told it from generation to generation as have the Jewish people. Jesus would hear the story of his people at home. It was the theme of the readings, prayers and sermons in the village Meeting House. This was what the scrolls – 'The Law' and 'The Prophets' – were all about. Jesus could see famous places in his people's story in the Galilean countryside. A short walk from his village led to the edge of the hills; and there, a thousand feet below him, lay the Esdraelon valley; it was like a scroll of history where village and hill and river recalled incidents and people of the past.

Away to the east rose Mount Tabor from which the highland tribes, one stormy day, had rushed down on the foreign cavalry struggling in the mud and water. To the southeast lay Gilboa Hill where King Saul had fought his last battle with the Philistines and committed suicide rather than surrender. Through the gap in the hills opposite ran the road to the south which went near the old city of Dothan where Joseph's brothers thought they had got rid of him. To the west the road rose through the Megiddo Pass where King Josiah died facing the Egyptian army. And beyond, where the hills lean to the sea was Mount Carmel, famous for the exploits of the prophet Elijah.

Everything spoke to him of his people's history.

He read the synagogue scrolls with care and imagination and insight – but found himself reading them in a way very different from the way in which the rabbis read them. It was common ground between himself and his countrymen that his people had been called to be 'God's People'. But what did that mean? What kind of people were 'God's People' to be? What was their job in the world?

These are the questions Jesus must have struggled with in the long years in Nazareth.

Two incidents were told about him which showed how he had to get clear what the 'leadership' of his people really meant.

The first is Jesus's call by God to be the leader of his people.
Here is Luke's account of it:

Crowds came to John to be baptised in the water of Jordan River. And
among them came Jesus.

He had been baptised and he was standing on the bank of the river,
praying.

Then it happened. From the open heavens, God's Spirit came down on
him, like a dove.

'You are my only Son,' said a voice from heaven. 'With you I am very well
pleased.'

The words Jesus heard in his heart come from a hymn which used
to be sung in the old days, at the king's coronation.

He must have been taken by surprise. He had gone down to the
Jordan River to join John the Baptist and his friends who were calling
the Jewish people to be ready for God's 'Chosen Leader' when God
sent him. Suddenly, Jesus realised God was calling him to be that
leader.

Jesus went away from Jordan River, his heart filled with God's Spirit. And
God led him out on to the lonely moorlands.

He was there many a long day. He was being tested; he had to think things
out; what did God want him to do? All this time he had nothing to eat, and
at the end he was very hungry indeed.

This conversation took place in his mind: Jesus imagined himself to be
sometimes on the moorlands themselves, sometimes on the top of a very high
mountain, sometimes standing on the top of the Temple Gate in Jerusalem.

On the moorlands:
Voice: If you are God's Son, tell this stone to become a loaf of bread.
Jesus: The Bible says: Bread is not the only thing a man needs to live on.

*On the top of a very high mountain, where he could see so far that all the world
seemed to lie at his feet:*
Voice: I will give you all the power of these great countries and their royal
splendour. It is all mine – mine to give to anybody I want to. It can all be
yours – on one condition: you must take me for your King – not God.
Jesus: The Bible says: God himself must be your King; you must be his
servant and his servant only.

*Jerusalem, on the top of the Temple Gate, looking down on all the people
gathered in the Court below:*
Voice: If you are God's Son jump down from this high place. The Bible
says: God will command his angels to look after you.

And again the Bible says: Their hands will hold you fast – you won't even stub your toe on a stone.

Jesus: The Bible also says: You must not put God to the test.

The testing time of Jesus was over – but it was not the last test he had to face.

He had long thought about what kind of leader God's 'Chosen Leader' would be. But it had not occurred to him that he himself would be called by God to be 'the leader of his people'. Now he knew that to be 'the leader of God's people' was the job God had given him to do. He had to make a final decision. He faced the great crisis of his life – but not the last crisis.

It was one thing to try to think things out in Nazareth; it was another to find himself shaken by a profound religious experience in which he believed God was, as it were, commissioning him for this great work. All he had read in the Old Testament, all he had become aware of in his own experience of God, all the ideas and convictions that had become clear in debate and argument with freedom-fighters and the rabbis met in one explosive moment.

What kind of work was his to be? Jesus went out into the lonely hills to pray and think things out.

The 'temptations' or 'testings' Jesus faced came from the different ways in which he could have been the leader of his people. He turned them all down. The words of refusal he used all come from the great 'Law Book' in the Old Testament (Deuteronomy) – a book he loved. It is as if he is saying 'No, that's not God's Way'.

The second incident is a mountain climb. Here is Mark's account of what happened:

Jesus took his three friends, Peter, James, and John, and led them up into a high mountain. They were alone.

High up the mountain, Jesus was changed.

His friends were still with him. His clothes were gleaming white; no bleacher on earth could make them whiter. His friends saw two other men talking with Jesus: Moses, who had led the people out of slavery in Egypt, and Elijah, who had stood up to a king in God's name.

Peter didn't know what to say, so he started talking like this.

'Sir,' he said. 'It's grand for us to be up here. Do you want us to make three shelters, one for you, one for Moses and one for Elijah?'

Peter and James and John were terrified.

A cloud rolled round them. God's words came into their minds.

'This is my only son. You must do as he says.'

The three men looked round. There was nobody there but Jesus.

As they went down the mountainside, Jesus told them not to talk about what they had seen to anybody, 'until I have risen from the dead'.

It was this saying they could not forget. They talked again and again among themselves about what 'rising from the dead' could mean.

We do not know what happened. But the three friends of Jesus shared his tremendous experience. Only a week before, when Peter had argued with Jesus, it was clear how little they understood him or had listened to what he was saying. So he took his three closest friends with him to try to help them to grasp what he knew was the way God's work should be done.

Perhaps it was on this mountain climb that he first told anybody about what happened at his 'Call' and his struggle in the loneliness of the hills (see p.69). He talked to them of Moses and Elijah – the great figures in the history of his people – and how it was their work he was called by God to carry on. But even after this great experience, they were still puzzled men.

The stories Jesus told are all about the work God had given him to do. They are full of echoes, sometimes actual quotations, from the Old Testament and they show what Jesus believed about God's 'Great Day'.

Here are three of his stories; in the first he quotes a poem of one of the prophets about 'God's Day'; the 'wild birds' in the Old Testament are used as a picture of 'foreign nations':

God's way is like this.
    When a mustard seed is sown in the soil, it's the smallest seed in the world. But it grows up and becomes the largest plant in the world. Its branches are so big that (you remember what the Bible says?)

> In the shelter of its branches
> the wild birds roost.

Once upon a time a rich man was giving a great feast, and he invited many guests.
    When the feast was ready, he sent his slave to all who were invited: 'Come along: it's all ready'.
    They all alike made excuses.
    'I've bought some land,' said the first. 'I must go out and look at it. Please excuse me.'
    'I've bought ten animals,' said another, 'and I'm going to test them. Please excuse me.'
    'I've just got married,' said another, 'I can't come.'
    The slave went back and told his master what they said. The master was angry.
    'Go out into the town at once,' he told his slave. 'Bring in the beggars and the cripples and the blind people and the lame people from the streets and alleyways.'

God's Way is like this.

A farmer went out sowing. He scattered the seed on the earth, and then didn't bother about it any more. Every day he got up and went on with his farmwork, and every night he went to bed and slept.

The days went by, and the seeds sprouted and grew tall. The farmer didn't know how it happened, but he knew what the soil itself could do: first there would be the green shoot, then the ear, then the ripe corn. But when the crop was ready (you remember what the Bible says?) –

> He puts in the sickle –
> harvest time's here.

Jesus is here dealing with his people's story and the decision they must now make. What he had to say is clearer in this story of a fig tree ('fig tree' in the Old Testament is a picture of the Jewish people):

A farmer had planted a fig tree in his vineyard. One day he went to look for figs on it; there were none.

'Look,' he said to his gardener. 'I've been coming here, looking for figs on this tree, for three years; I haven't found a single one. Why should it waste good ground?'

'Sir,' said the gardener, 'let it alone for another year. I'll dig the earth round it and put manure on it. If there are figs on the tree next year – that will be fine. If not, you can cut it down.'

But it is clearest in this story of how John the Baptist sent two of his friends to Jesus. Note that Jesus gives as his answer a quotation from the Old Testament (the Isaiah Scroll):

One day the hermit John, who was in prison, called two of his friends and sent them to Jesus to ask him a question.

'John has sent us to you,' they told Jesus when they met him. 'He wants to know if you are the Great Deliverer God promised to send us, or must we go on waiting for somebody else?'

There was a crowd of people with Jesus that day; he was making many sick people better and giving many blind people the power to see.

'Go back to John,' he said to the two men, 'and tell him what you have seen and heard. You remember what the Bible says?'

Here Jesus quotes words from the Old Testament which describe what 'God's Great Day' will be like and how then men and women will be set free from all the evil and suffering which are now their lot (see Isaiah 29: 18–19, 35: 5–6 and 61: 1).

'Blind people see again;
  lame people walk about;
lepers are made better;
  deaf people are hearing;
dead people are alive again;
  hopeless people are told the Good News.

The really happy man is the man who isn't shocked at what I am doing.'

The narrowness and self-concern of his countrymen (which his own friends shared) troubled Jesus most. The freedom-fighters did not, indeed, represent most of the Jewish people; but even those who did not share their violent dreams thought of themselves as a closed community and the rest of the world as outside God's concern unless they became Jews.

Jesus believed that all the world was God's world and all its people his concern.

There was an Old Testament story Jesus particularly loved – he quoted it more than once. It was not a story that the extreme nationalists or the Pharisees liked. It tells how the capital city of the bitterest enemies of the Jewish people – the enemies who had destroyed Jerusalem – changed their minds when Jonah preached to them and were accepted by God. It's a story Jesus himself could have told.

Once upon a time God spoke to Jonah.

'Get up,' he said, 'and go to that great city, Nineveh. Pronounce its doom – its shameful wickedness has been reported to me.'

Jonah set off – but he made for Tartessus in the far west, right away from God. He went down to the port of Joppa. There was a large cargo-boat in the harbour. He paid his passage and went on board; he didn't want to have anything to do with God and his commands.

Out at sea they ran into a hurricane. The sea was so rough that the ship seemed about to break up. The sailors were in a panic, each shouting out to his own god for help. They threw the cargo overboard to lighten the ship.

Jonah had gone down into the hold, and was lying there fast asleep. The captain went down to see what he was doing.

'What do you mean by sleeping like this?' he shouted. 'Get up and pray to your God. He might take some notice of us and come to our help.'

Meanwhile the sailors were talking together.

'Let's toss up,' they were saying, 'and find out who's to blame for this bad luck.'

They tossed up – and it was Jonah.

'Tell us your business,' they said. 'Where do you come from? What's your country? Who are your people?'

'I'm a Hebrew,' he told them. 'I'm running away from God – the God of heaven who made the sea and the land.'

'What a thing to do!' they said. 'What shall we do with you to quieten the storm?'

The sea was growing rougher and rougher.

'Throw me overboard,' said Jonah. 'That will calm the sea. I know I am to blame for this hurricane.'

But the men didn't throw him overboard. They rowed as hard as they could to get the ship into harbour. All in vain – the sea grew stormier and stormier still.

Then they prayed to Jonah's God:

'O God,' they prayed, 'don't let us die if we throw this man overboard; don't hold it against us. The storm is your doing.'

Then they threw Jonah overboard – and the storm died down.

The sailors were filled with awe in God's presence: they worshipped him and vowed to serve him.

God sent a great fish. It swallowed Jonah, and there he stayed inside the fish, for three whole days. He then ordered the fish to put Jonah on shore, and it vomited him out on to the dry land.

God spoke to Jonah a second time.

'Get up and go to the great city, Nineveh,' he repeated, 'and pronounce its doom, as I shall tell you.'

This time Jonah got up and went to Nineveh as God ordered him.

Now Nineveh was a large city. To walk across it, from city wall to city wall, was a three days' walk. Jonah entered the city and walked for a whole day. He stood and announced its doom.

'In forty days' time,' he shouted, 'this city will become a heap of ruins!'

The citizens of Nineveh at once accepted God's word. All of them – from the greatest nobleman to the poorest worker – covered themselves with sackcloth and sat down in grief.

News of all this reached the royal palace. The king got up from his throne and stripped off his royal robes. He, too, put on sackcloth and sat down in grief.

He issued a proclamation and the heralds carried it through the city:

BY ORDER OF THE KING AND HIS MINISTERS!

A FAST IS PROCLAIMED FOR ALL CITIZENS AND ALL ANIMALS. NOTHING SHALL BE EATEN AND NOTHING DRUNK. ALL SHALL PUT ON SACKCLOTH AND PRAY TO GOD WITH THEIR WHOLE HEART. EVERY CITIZEN SHALL TURN FROM HIS EVIL WAYS AND FROM EVERY ACT OF VIOLENCE.

'Who knows?' thought the king. 'God may yet change his mind, and stop being angry with us; the city may be saved.

Indeed, when God saw what they had done – how they had given up all their evil ways – he changed his mind. He did not destroy the city.

Jonah was very angry indeed.

'Isn't this just what I said would happen when I was back at home?' he said to God. 'That's why I ran away to the west. I know the sort of God you are – "Kind and merciful, slow to anger, quick to love men with all your heart", as the hymn [See Psalms 86.15; 103.8; 145.8 (also Exodus 34.6)] says. I knew you would change your mind. I'd rather be dead than alive.'

'Is anger all you can think of?' asked God.

Jonah just walked out of the East Gate of the city and sat down to see what would happen.

God made a plant grow up to shade his head – the great heat of the sun was too much for him. That made Jonah happier. But at dawn, next day, a worm attacked the plant and it died. The sun rose, a scorching east wind blew and the heat beat down on Jonah. He nearly fainted.

'I'd rather be dead than alive!' he groaned.

'Is being angry like this right?' asked God.

'It is!' said Jonah. 'I could die with anger!'

'But Jonah,' said God, 'you are sorry for a plant which grew up in a night and died in a night – a plant you hadn't done anything for, and which grew without your help. Shouldn't I be sorry for the great city of Nineveh (even if it is a foreign city) with its hundred and twenty thousand ignorant people – and its animals?'

Here are Jesus's comments on that story:

> The people of Nineveh will stand up in God's Great Day
>   and show how blind people today are:
> when they heard Jonah, they listened and changed their ways.
>   Look! Something much more important than Jonah is here.

What he began

Jesus faced an immensely difficult task.

Against him were the violent propaganda of the freedom-fighters and the power of established religion – its leaders and institutions. Jesus was the critic of them all – the way they lived, what they thought the story of their people was about and what most people thought was the heart of religion itself.

He took his stand on his deepest convictions, and he gave himself to the outcasts of his society. But there was more to be done.

He believed he had been sent to carry on what God had been doing in the story of his people. But what could he do if both people and government would not listen? Jesus had hoped that they would. But they didn't.

When it was clear that they would not, he began to call into being a new community who would really be God's People, live in God's Way and be God's fellow-workers. He gathered round him a group of friends. Many of these friends went on living in their own villages; some of them became his close friends and joined him to help him in his work.

This is Mark's account of the first close friends Jesus called:

One day Jesus was walking along the seashore; he saw Peter and his brother Andrew casting their nets into the sea – they were fishermen.

'Come with me,' said Jesus. 'I'll show you better fishing than this – for men, not fish.'

And they left their nets and went with him.

A little farther on James and his brother John were getting their nets ready in the boat. Jesus called them, and they left their father with his men in the boat and went away with him.

Some time later Jesus was again out walking and he saw Levi at work in the tax office.

'Come with me,' said Jesus.

Levi got up and went with him.

He gave his close friends a special name – 'The Twelve'. The word goes back to the early days of the Hebrew people, when they settled in Palestine as their homeland and organised themselves as a League of Twelve Tribes. Jesus's close friends were to be the new 'Twelve', called, as it were, to begin the history of their people again with Jesus as their Leader, and to live as the real People of God.

Before we read the story of how Jesus chose his close friends and called them 'The Twelve', we ought to remember how important the story of The Twelve Tribes was in the history of his people. It is told in the Old Testament books Exodus, Joshua and Judges (*Winding Quest*, 'Memories of the Past', pp.88ff). It was a dangerous story. Jesus never hid from 'The Twelve' that theirs would be a dangerous story too.

Jesus went into the hills and called the men he wanted and they went out to him. He chose a small company of very close friends, and he called them the 'Twelve'.

He wanted them to be with him, and to go out telling the Good News about God and making sick people better.

These are the 'Twelve' and some of the nicknames Jesus gave them:

Simon 'Rock' (we say 'Peter')
James and John, the sons of Zebedee 'Thunder and Lightning'
Andrew
Philip
Bartholomew
Matthew
James, the son of Alphaeus
Thomas
Thaddeus
Simon 'Rebel'
Judas (Judas was called 'Iscariot' like his father; this is the friend who handed Jesus over to the Jewish Government.)

Jesus sent the Twelve out, two by two, into the villages; and he gave them power to make sick people better.

His orders were: 'Travel light with staff and sandals, no food, no bag, no money in your belt, and only one shirt.'

Their orders were clear: they were to be Jesus's 'apprentices', telling people (as he did) the Good News about God and caring for the sick and outcast.

We have seen how slow his friends were to grasp what he was talking about and what he was trying to do. He didn't expect them to grasp it all at once. He knew only too well how strong were the popular ideas about 'being God's People', and what a break with them his friends would have to make. He put it in these words:

> You don't sew a patch of new cloth
>   on an old dress.
> If you do, the new patch
>   pulls at the old dress.
> Then you've got a worse tear.
>
> You don't put new wine
>   into old wine-skins.
> If you do, the wine bursts the skins
>   and wine and skins are lost.
> New wine-skins for new wine!

Jesus had not called them just to be his individual friends; he had called them to be a new kind of community. Anybody could become a member of it, whatever his race or education or background. Membership would rest on loyalty to God alone; its members would be committed to live in God's Way.

The new community would not be founded on force. It would be a caring community whose members were to be ready to be the servants of men and women because they were God's servants. Their job was not 'to win adherents for a cause – to enlist recruits, let us say, for the army of God, to enrol workers who will begin to build the kingdom of God on earth, to mobilise all the available man-power in support of God's enterprises'. Their job was to be a 'servant community', as Jesus himself was just the servant of both God and men and women. They were to live, as he did, for those nobody wants, the outcast and the helpless: 'I didn't come to have servants looking after me' Jesus must have said many times. 'I came to be a servant myself and to give myself to make everybody free.'

There are three 'images' or 'pictures' which Jesus used to describe himself and his new community and how they were to live in the wide world of nations and peoples. We must take them quite seriously.

They are yeast, salt and daylight:

> God's Way is like this:
>   A woman took some yeast and mixed it into a lot
> of flour; and *all* the flour rose.
>
> Salt is good.
> But what can you do with salt that is no longer salty?
> It's fit neither for food nor for manure.
> You can only throw it into the street.
>
> You, who are my friends, are like daylight; you must help
> people to see everything clearly.

You cannot make a loaf of yeast, but you can't make a loaf without it.

You cannot make a dinner of salt, but salt makes food worth eating.

Daylight doesn't tell you where to go; it enables you to walk without stumbling and to see where you are going.

God is at work everywhere in the whole world of men and women, and he is in charge. The community of Jesus's friends is here to help in the making of his world, and they do so by living in his Way, ready for any job anywhere, any time. This is what it means to be 'God's fellow-workers'.

Jesus summed it up in his most important poem:

> Love your enemies,
>   do good to those who hate you,
>   bless those who curse you,
>   pray for those who treat you badly.
>
> If you love those who love you,
>   what is there special about that?
>   Everybody does that sort of thing.
> If you favour those who favour you,
>   what is there special about that?
>   Everybody does that sort of thing.
> If you lend money to those you hope will help you,
>   what is there special about that?
>   Everybody does that sort of thing.
>
> Love your enemies;
>   do good and lend,
>   expecting nothing back.

You *will* get something back:
    you will be living in God's Way –
        he is kind to those who never say 'Thank you',
        and to those who are selfishness itself.

Be merciful
    as God your Father is merciful.

Don't judge and you won't be judged;
    don't condemn and you won't be condemned;
forgive and you will be forgiven;
    give and you will be given;
        good measure,
        pressed down,
        shaken together,
        running over,
        will be poured into your lap.

The measure you give
    will be the measure you get.

The price to be paid

Jesus never hid from his friends the danger in which they all stood and the price they might have to pay for the stand they were making.

His friends may not have really listened to him when he talked like this. They may have been so convinced (as many of their fellow-countrymen were) that God would act in some dramatic, spectacular way to establish his 'kingdom' that the idea of God's 'Chosen Leader' suffering was unthinkable. It would be his enemies who would suffer. This was what was probably in Peter's mind when he rebuked Jesus on the country road (see pp.42–3).

Jesus was no dreamer. He knew the kind of world in which he was living. He knew too, from the Old Testament, how the prophets had been treated. In his own day, the man under whom his own work for God had been begun, John the Baptist, had died a violent death in one of King Herod's prisons. He could have been under no illusion about what his fate might finally be.

He had to face all kinds of hostility:

One day, in Galilee, some Jewish Leaders came to Jesus.
    'You'd better get out of here,' they said. 'King Herod's after you.'
    'This is what I've got to say to that "fox", and you can tell him,' said

Jesus. 'I shall go on doing what I have been doing, healing people who are sick in mind or body – today and tomorrow and the day after. I shall finish the work God has given me to do. A man of God is in no danger – outside Jerusalem City.'

This happened in Samaria. Jesus was on his way south to Jerusalem City.

He sent friends on ahead to find somewhere to spend the night. They came to a village, but the villagers turned them out, for one reason only – Jesus and his friends, it was obvious, were on their way to Jerusalem, the Holy City of their hated enemies.

'Sir,' said James and John, when they heard this, 'You remember what happened when Elijah was turned away from a village – fire came down from the sky and burned the villagers up. Do you want us to ask God to burn these villagers up?'

Jesus turned round and stopped such talk; and they went on to another village.

There can be no doubt that, certainly in the last months of his life, Jesus talked about the kind of death neither he nor probably his friends would be able to escape. Something like this must have often happened in those last days:

Jesus and the 'Twelve' were on the road going up to Jerusalem. Jesus was striding on ahead; his friends were following behind him, alarmed and frightened.

Jesus took them on one side again, and told them what was going to happen to him.

'Look,' he said, 'we're going up to Jerusalem, the capital city. I shall be handed over to the Jewish Leaders, and they will want to put me to death. That means handing me over to the Romans, who won't be very gentle in the way they treat me; they will kill me. But, as I have told you, my death will not be the end. I shall soon "rise".'

Jesus meant business. He did not come just to talk. To *talk* about God as Abba, Father, was not enough. That God was Abba was for Jesus the very foundation of the world. It was the central truth that made sense of the strange and bewildering story of the human race. It was the clue – and the only clue – he had. He lived in the light of it and he was to die because he would not go back on it. From the very beginning he was prepared to pay the price of his convictions.

Jesus meant business; he intended to change human society. He wanted to awaken men to the truth about the world in which they were living. God was at work, and it was God's world that was being made; that was the fact that men had to reckon with. There was no other way.

His own work, he believed, was to take a decisive part in God's making of the world. God was actually changing the whole structure of human society through the work he was doing.

The Jewish government and the freedom-fighters realised that they were dealing with someone they could not ignore, and who, if he really captured the imagination of the whole people, would turn their world upside-down.

Yet, in all this, Jesus was not concerned about himself; he was concerned with what God was doing. He was ready to be the servant of his fellow-men. It is here that Jesus shows himself very different from all other leaders. They set themselves up as leaders and make all sorts of claims for themselves. But, as one scholar puts it, 'Jesus did not make claims for himself, nor was he in the least interested in his own security'.

Yet he possessed a strange authority – and he claimed a loyalty few leaders have demanded. It was the truth for which he stood that gave him that authority, not any claim he made for himself. It was the truth that ought to be plain to everybody – as plain as the changes in the weather. The test of that truth was not in himself. It was not true because he said it – its truth was to be seen in the fruits of his work and the effect of what he was doing:

> No healthy tree
>   grows rotten fruit;
> no rotten tree
>   grows healthy fruit.
> You can tell every tree by its fruit:
>   from a thorn-bush you don't get figs;
>   from a bramble-bush you don't get grapes.
>
> The good man out of the richness of a good heart
>   grows goodness;
> the evil man out of an evil heart
>   grows evil.

All that Jesus had when he came face to face with the hostility of the Jewish government and the might of Rome was his conviction that God had given him his work to do and that he must use the authority he believed had been given him for the outcast and the helpless. That was all.

God would vindicate him – of that Jesus had no doubt – and would vindicate him in no uncertain way. When? Jesus didn't know. But he did know what he had to face:

> I came to set the world on fire –
>   how I wish the fire were burning now!
> Mine is a dangerous life;
>   how hard it will be for me until my work is done!
> Do you think it is 'peace' I have come to give the world?
>   I tell you No – the very opposite of 'peace'!

Who, then, can this be?

We pause to look back on what we have been learning about Jesus from his friends and contemporaries, and to ask the question, before we go any further, 'What, at this point, do we make of him?'.

There is one important point to note before we begin to answer this question. We have been talking about Jesus in a twentieth century way and in twentieth century language. This, of course, is the only way we can talk about anyone, whether they are our contemporaries or lived a long time ago. But if they lived a long time ago, there is a danger we have to be aware of. The danger is that we begin to think of them as if they were twentieth century people like us, and forget that they were living in a very different world from ours. Whether we are talking of Jesus (as we are now) or of someone like Socrates or Julius Caesar, we must always remember that they were people of their own centuries. They spoke and thought in the language and with the knowledge and assumptions and ways of their own time.

Jesus was a Jew of first century Palestine. He spoke the Galilean dialect of Aramaic. He thought as other first century Jewish people did. We live on this side of a great revolution in human thought – the rise of modern science and the birth of the modern world. Jesus lived far on the other side of it.

The people of his day thought of the universe as (by our modern standards) a very small place with a very brief history. They knew nothing of what we would call the 'laws of nature' which makes possible the enquiries, discoveries and explanations of modern scientists. Their ideas of how the world 'works' were inherited from the past and were not given any kind of critical examination, such as modern scientists would give them. Their knowledge of past history was not based on the kind of research a modern historian would undertake.

But different as the world of the first century was from ours today and in spite of the vast changes that have taken place, *people* haven't changed – as we can see if we compare the world of our own experience and of the stories we read in our newspapers with the world of the stories Jesus told. The villages and towns have changed; the people who live in them have not. We can recognise today the world of Jesus's stories – we meet his 'characters' everywhere.

The people of Jesus's time were not fools. They could ask very shrewd questions. There were many who would not take what was reported at its face value but would say (as Herodotus, the Greek historian who lived about the time of Nehemiah, in the fifth century B.C. said) 'I merely repeat the tradition – I do not myself believe it'. Inherited beliefs and assumptions could be debated and challenged or rejected or re-interpreted – in Palestine as well as in Greece (see a prophet like Amos or a poet like the author of Job: *Winding Quest* pp.232–244; 257–269).

There was a widespread belief in demons – 'evil spirits' – and demon-possession; indeed, much illness was explained in this way, especially illnesses like epilepsy or madness. Many stories were told about demons and their influence on men, and about 'exorcists' (people who 'cast out demons') and their achievements. The belief that evil spirits cause illness is still widespread in many parts of the world today. Jesus was talking about demon-possession in his ghost story:

Once upon a time a ghost lived in a haunted house. At last he was driven out. He wandered through the dry desert looking for somewhere to make his home. He had no luck.

'I'm going back to the old house,' said he.

So he went back, and there was the old house, swept clean and freshly decorated – and empty!

Off he went again, and brought seven other ghosts, much worse than himself, to live with him. They all settled down there together. Things in that house were far worse than they had ever been before.

This can happen to us.

Jesus himself was widely thought of as an exorcist and his healings are often described in the stories of his friends as 'casting out demons':

'We saw a man making sick people better (casting out demons) and using your name,' said John to Jesus one day. 'He doesn't belong to us, so we stopped him.'

'Don't stop him,' said Jesus. 'Nobody will do a good deed, as one of my friends, and then quickly insult me. If a man is not our enemy, he is our friend. If anybody gives you a cup of water as a friend of mine, because you are doing God's work, I am very sure he won't miss his place in God's Kingdom.'

It was also a time when people believed in 'magic' and 'miracle' and got these very much mixed up. A person who believed in magic believed that 'non-human, superhuman, usually invisible powers, including the gods themselves, the angelic beings, demons of various orders and the souls of heroes and men' are linked somehow 'with material things like plants, minerals, animals, times and seasons, human beings'. They also believed that if you know all about this sort of thing and could use this knowledge, you could make these super-human powers do what you want – hurt people through a curse or cure people through speaking a special name. There are stories in the New Testament about people who claimed to be able to work cures this way. Here is one (it happened in Ephesus):

There were seven Jewish travelling doctors, sons of a Jewish leader called Sceva. They heard about Paul, and began to use the words he used – 'In the name of Jesus' – as their magic words.

'I am speaking to you,' they would say to a sick person, 'in the name of the Jesus whom Paul talks about.'

They went to a house, one day (so the story ran) to heal a sick man who believed an evil spirit was inside him. They used, as they had often done before, the words 'in the name of Jesus whom Paul talks about'.

But this time the spirit inside the man suddenly shouted out.

'I know who Jesus is,' it shouted, 'and I know who Paul is. But who are you?'

The sick man jumped on them, knocked them about and was so violent that they ran out of the house naked and badly beaten up.

'Miracle' is not the same as 'magic', though many people, now as then, mix the two up. A miracle is not an event which necessarily violates the order and pattern which scientific research has discovered in the world about us. It was certainly a wonderful act of God to people of the ancient world; but they knew nothing, as we have said, of our modern scientific way of ordering our experience – there were no 'natural laws' for them to think of God as 'breaking' them. The word 'miracle' has nothing essentially to do with anything spectacular and incredible; it is simply an event in which we become aware of God's presence. Here is a twentieth century definition of the word 'miracle': 'an event which through its unusual character attracts our attention, but also awakens or deepens our awareness of, our faith in, and our assurance of, the love of God'. In the New Testament the word corresponding to the popular meaning of 'miracle' ('wonder') is rarely used; the common words used to describe the 'miracles' of Jesus are 'power' and 'sign'.

How, then, do we set about getting clear what kind of man Jesus was?

We must, first, place him in his world. We must not expect that words and ways of talking in the first century mean just what we would now mean by the same words and ways of talking. For example, there may or may not be such a thing as 'demon-possession'. That is a matter for research and discussion in the light of all our present-day knowledge. But in the time of Jesus it would be a natural way of describing all sorts of diseases – epilepsy, mental illness and those diseases where modern doctors are aware of how much body affects mind and mind affects body. Jesus shared the medical knowledge of his time.

Secondly, we must sort out the evidence. As we have seen, there are many different kinds of stories about him – popular stories, stories which go back to eyewitnesses, preachers' stories. Stories always grow in the telling and we have to remember that the first friends of Jesus shared the common love of the miraculous which was very strong in the first century. So the stories need sorting out and weighing up.

Thirdly, we must note exactly what happened. We must note that Jesus (who was often thought of in Jewish and pagan circles in later years as a magician) did not emphasise his healings or call attention to them; indeed, on one occasion, as we have seen, when he thought people were thinking more about his healings than about what he was saying, he refused to go back to them, and went off elsewhere to 'tell the good news' about God (see p.59). He thought of his healings as showing God's power at work, but not as strange and magical events – or as the proof of who he was.

Fourthly, we must remember that what Jesus was and what he did and said were not so different and strange that we cannot be expected to understand him two thousand years later. His character shines through all the reports we have of him; and the fact that he put what he had to say in stories and poems has given them the power to speak, as all art does, across the centuries, and across the great changes in human thought and culture. There are aspects of Jesus which we shall perhaps never quite understand and words of his whose meaning will always escape us. But the central thing for which he stood and the kind of man he was are not in doubt. So a great artist like Rembrandt can read the New Testament sixteen hundred years later and paint pictures and make etchings of the stories he found there in such a way that, as we look at them in the Rijksmuseum in Amsterdam, Jesus faces us with the same challenge and the same 'good news' with which he faced people and challenged them in Galilee.

The real 'miracle' about Jesus, then and now, is that he made God real to those who took him seriously and became his friends. Jesus made God real for Paul who once wrote to some friends: 'God, who made this bright world, has filled my heart with light, the light which shines now I know what he is really like. This was the light which was shining from the face of Jesus'.

This is the real 'miracle' of Jesus. This is what he has meant to his friends whatever century they have lived in and to whatever culture they have belonged and whatever scientific view of the world they have felt compelled to hold.

And so, alongside the words of first-century Paul, we can put the words of a twentieth-century scientist: 'Once one has really looked at the Jesus of the Gospels and really seen him and the role he is taking and what is regarded as having happened to him, he is an inescapable element . . . in all one's future thinking about both the . . . reality of God and the nature of man.'

The Outcome

Road to Jerusalem

The turning point in Jesus's public career seems to have been the incident when he met the men of the Resistance Movement, the 'incident in the hills', as we have called it (see pp.7–8).

There must have been something strong and commanding about Jesus that made freedom-fighters think of him as a possible leader, the kind of man they thought should be their 'king'. The day they met him in a lonely spot out of reach of the Roman garrison at Capernaum brought matters to a head.

We can see how they came to think about him as they did. There was his note of authority. He was acting as though he believed he had been called to lead the Jewish people. His theme was 'God's Rule' ('The Kingdom of God') – the slogan of the freedom-fighters. What became dramatically clear that day in the hills was that Jesus and the freedom-fighters were poles apart. He had no use for a 'Holy War' and all the bitter violence which such a war would mean – and which, in a few years, became a reality when war broke out between the Jewish people and the Roman legions. Jesus did not think of foreigners as they did. When what Jesus really stood for dawned on them, they had no further use for him. Indeed, many of the people who had thought of themselves as his friends abandoned him. Jesus seems to have had to face the last months of his life almost alone. Very few of his friends stood by him. Even they, at the last dangerous moment, when soldiers were arresting him in the orchard, ran away.

But it was a crisis, also, it seems, for Jesus. Soon after, he left Galilee. When he passed through it again on his way to the south, he travelled incognito: he didn't want anybody to recognise him.

What Jesus had to face was the failure (as it must have seemed to him) of all he had been doing in Galilee. The final impression he seems to have made on his fellow-Galileans was that of a lost leader – a man to be dropped with contempt by the men everybody admired. He had, of course, long been disliked and opposed by many of the religious leaders in the synagogues. All he was left with now was a handful of friends.

He had to re-examine his work. We saw in the story of the incident on the road near Caesarea Philippi and the mountain climb with his three friends, a few months after the incident in the hills (see pages 42–3, 71) how his call at the Jordan River was in his mind. Ought he to have done his work differently?

He came to the conclusion that there was no other way in which the work to which God had called him could be done. He had lived in God's way and called his countrymen to live in God's way; that was all he could do. He set his face to go south, to the capital city, Jerusalem. He must begin there the same work he had been doing in Galilee.

He knew the dangers which he would now face. Jerusalem was the headquarters of the Jewish Government; and there the Roman Governor himself, representative of the power of Rome, was in final charge.

It seems that Jesus had made up his mind to appeal to his people at the Passover Festival when the temple would be crowded with Jewish pilgrims from Palestine and from all parts of the world. He would speak his final word to his people.

He set off south. He seems to have arrived in Jerusalem in October at the time of the Festival of Tents. He spoke in the Temple Courts (as it was the habit of Jewish teachers to do) and here he came into conflict with the Temple authorities. It was now obvious to them that he was a threat to all they believed; they made up their minds to get rid of him.

There are two events which happened when Jesus and his friends reached the city in October. He had deliberately planned them. They have been called 'acted parables' and they were intended to make clear in action, as his stories made clear in words, what he really stood for. The first seems to have been addressed to his friends; the second (to which we have already referred – p.46) was addressed to the religious leaders and the Temple authorities, the government of his people.

The first incident happened on the road into the city itself, when Jesus and his friends joined the worshipping pilgrims who had come up the steep road from Jericho and were singing hymns as they walked along. It was the great autumn festival when the people lived in temporary tents or 'booths', remembering the joy of harvest and the coming of the new year, but also celebrating their march through the desert from Egypt to their homeland.[1] As the pilgrims came in sight of the city they began to recite the words of a hymn:

[1] See *Winding Quest* pp.102–117.

This is our prayer, O God:
  rescue us!
  give us victory!
Happy is he who comes in God's name!
  We send you happiness from God's house!

Jesus used the occasion to bring home to his friends again – friends who still shared many of the nationalistic aims of the day – that he came in peace and not for war. Did Jesus remember that time, centuries before, when his great ancestor, King David, rode into the city, after a great battle, on his warhorse at the head of his soldiers? Jesus rode into his capital city, not on a horse, but on a donkey, an ordinary farm animal, borrowed from a friend. It must have been a private act for his friends, and not, as Christians later thought of it, a public march of triumph. When later the government at his trial was looking for any evidence that could be used to make him look like a revolutionary who ought to be executed, nobody suggested this ride into the city. Here is the way the story was told in Christian circles:

Jerusalem was at last in sight. Near the Olive Hill, Jesus sent his friends to a village.

'Go into the village facing you,' Jesus said, 'and just as you go in you'll find a donkey. It'll be tied up, and it hasn't been broken in yet. Untie it and bring it; and if anyone asks you why you are doing this, tell them: "The Master needs it, and he'll send it straight back".'

They set off, and found the donkey tied at a door outside in the street. They untied it.

'What are you untying the donkey for?' asked some of the bystanders.

They said what Jesus had told them to say, and the men let them take it away.

They brought the donkey to Jesus and threw their clothes on its back. Jesus sat on it. People spread their clothes on the road, and others put leafy branches from the fields and spread them out. All the crowd, those in front and those behind, shouted the words from the old Bible hymn:

Hurrah!
Happy is he who comes in God's name!
Happy is the kingdom of King David, our father!
A thousand times – Hurrah!

If the ride into the city was a private gesture to his friends, the second 'acted parable' was in the full public gaze in the Foreigners' Court of the Temple.

We have already described how Jesus made it plain, in a public act of protest, that God's care was for all people (see p.46). We note now how he quoted some bitter words from two of the great prophets in the Old Testament. Here is Mark's account of this second 'acted parable':

Jesus walked into the city again and went into the Temple. In the great Foreigners' Court he drove out the shopkeepers who had their stalls there and the people who were buying. He upset the tables of the moneylenders and the chairs of the pigeon-sellers. He wouldn't let anybody take a short cut and carry goods through the Temple.

'Doesn't the Bible say,' he said, ' "My House shall be called the House of Worship for all foreign people"? You have made it a bandits' den.'

That sealed his doom.

'The Jewish leaders,' Mark tells us, 'now made up their minds to arrest Jesus.'

Jesus had challenged their central convictions: 'You have often heard, in the synagogue, the law [of Moses] read aloud,' he said, 'but I say . . .' He was making radical claims about the Jewish way of life and the leadership of the Jewish people. The clash between them was bitter and unrelenting. They laid their plans for his arrest.

Jesus, however, kept out of their reach. He spent the winter in the countryside east of Jordan River where their writ did not run. He came back to the city just before the Passover Festival in the spring. The authorities were waiting for him. Their plans were laid. He was arrested in the darkness of the night in an orchard outside the city on the Bethany road.

Death in the afternoon

What happened at the end is best told in the words the friends of Jesus used when week by week they remembered him in their worship.

They used to meet 'on the first day of the week' (the day when Jesus was 'raised from the dead') and have supper together. At the end of the supper, they repeated what Jesus had done on the last night, the night when he was arrested: they passed the common cup round and shared the common loaf together. Our earliest account of what Jesus did at supper comes from Paul; here are his words:

On the night when he was arrested, Jesus had supper with his friends. During supper he picked up the loaf of bread, said Grace over it and broke it in pieces.

'This is my very self,' he said. 'I am giving myself up for you. Do this to remember me by.'

When supper was over, he raised the cup in the same way.

'This cup,' he said, 'means my death. I am dying to bring all men to God, as the Bible says, "from the least of them to the greatest". Whenever you drink it, remember me.'

At some moment in their meeting, the story of how Jesus died was told.

Here is the account which the Christians in Italy used in their worship and which Mark copied down when he came, in his own account of Jesus, to describe what happened on that last night.

It happened two days before the Great Feast.

The Jewish Leaders were trying to find some way of getting hold of Jesus and killing him. They did not dare to do this openly, or when the Great Feast was on, for they were afraid of a riot.

They were delighted when they heard that one of the 'Twelve', Judas Iscariot, had come and offered to put Jesus into their hands. They promised to pay him, and Judas began to look out for the chance of doing it.

It was dark when Jesus and his friends came into the city.

'I tell you,' said Jesus, when they were having supper together, 'that one of you will betray me – one who is having supper with me now.'

His friends were hurt at this.

'It can't be me?' they each said to him.

'It's one of the "Twelve",' said Jesus. 'He is sharing this very meal with me. . . . What is going to happen is just what the Bible said would happen. But it will be a terrible thing for the man who betrays me; it would have been better for him if he had never lived.'

When supper was over, they sang a hymn; then they walked out to the Olive Hill outside the City, on the road to the village where he was staying.

'You will all let me down,' said Jesus, as they walked along. 'The Bible says:

> I will strike the shepherd
> and the sheep will run away.

But after I am "raised", I will go to Galilee before you.'

'Everybody else may let you down,' said Peter, 'but I won't.'

'I tell you, Peter,' said Jesus, 'that this very night, before dawn, you will say more than once that you're no friend of mine.'

'Say I'm no friend of yours?' said Peter hotly. 'I'd die with you first!'

Everybody else said the same.

They got as far as the Olive Orchard.

Suddenly, Judas came with a gang armed with swords and clubs. They had been sent by the Jewish Leaders. Judas had arranged a secret signal so that there should be no mistake.

'The man I kiss, that's Jesus,' he told them. 'Get hold of him, and take him away under guard.'

He went straight up to Jesus.

'Sir,' he said, and kissed him – as if he was just meeting him.

The men grabbed Jesus, and put him under guard, and took him to the High Court.

Early in the morning, the Jewish Council talked over what they should do with Jesus. They handcuffed him and took him off and handed him over to Pilate, the Roman Governor.

They brought charge after charge against him.

'Haven't you got anything to say?' asked Pilate. 'See the charges they are making against you.'

But Jesus had nothing more to say. Pilate was very surprised. He wanted to put the mob in a good mood, so he set Barabbas free and had Jesus flogged. Then he handed him over to the soldiers to be put to death on a cross.

Simon, whose home was in North Africa, was coming into the city from the country at the time. The soldiers made him carry the wooden cross and marched Jesus to Skull Hill. They offered him drugs to deaden the pain, but he didn't take them. They nailed him to the cross and tossed up for his clothes and shared them out among themselves.

The charge against Jesus was fastened on the cross, THE JEWISH KING.
Passers-by shook their heads and swore at Jesus.

'Aha! You'd pull the Temple down and rebuild it just like that? You'd
better look after yourself and get down from the cross!'

It was now three o'clock in the afternoon.

'My God, my God, why have you abandoned me?' Jesus called out loudly.
The words are the words of an old Bible hymn.

Some of those standing near heard him call out, but they did not catch the
words.

'See,' they said, 'he's calling for Elijah!'

One of them ran and filled a sponge with sour wine and put it on the end of
a cane and tried to make Jesus drink it.

'Let's see if Elijah comes to help him down!' they shouted to one another.

Jesus gave a loud cry and died.

The Roman officer in charge of the guard was standing facing Jesus and
saw how he died.

'This man was a real king!' he said.

It was now near sunset when the Holy Day of the Jews began, and all
preparation for any kind of work had to be finished.

There was a good man called Joseph, a well-known member of the Jewish
Council, from the village of Arimathea. He was brave enough to go to Pilate
and ask for the body of Jesus.

Pilate was very surprised to hear that Jesus was already dead. He ordered
the Commanding Officer to bring his report; when he heard the report from
the officer, he gave the body to Joseph.

Joseph took the body of Jesus down from the cross and wrapped it in a
linen sheet which he had brought. He put the body in a cave which had
already been cut out of the rock and rolled a stone against the mouth.

As we read this account we should remember three things.

The first is that this is not a piece of historical writing. It is part of an
act of worship. His friends were thinking, as they heard it read, of the
greatness of God's love which Jesus's death had made real for them.
It was never intended to be a detailed account of what happened.

The second thing is that when this account was written down there
was both misunderstanding and bitterness between the Jewish and
Christian communities. The account, as we now have it, emphasises
the Jewish part in Jesus's death (not the people's, but the Temple
authorities' part) and underestimates the part played by the Roman
governor, Pilate. There is no doubt that Pilate took the decisive
decision; he could hardly have done otherwise. Any suggestion that

there was a threat to Roman peace – especially in the crowded days of high festival – would force a Roman governor to act and to act quickly. The fact that Jesus's friends carried weapons on that night would settle the matter. Jesus was executed by the Roman governor as 'The King of the Jews' – the words of the charge fastened to the cross which he refused to alter or remove.

Finally, the death of Jesus came to mean to his friends, not a great miscarriage of justice over which to brood, but the celebration of God's love. This was the length to which Jesus's love of men and women took him. It was his resolution to live in God's Way and to call his people to live in God's Way that took him to his death. He could have escaped; he didn't try to.

So, at the end of the supper, he did something which he had never done before at any of their common meals – he passed the loaf and the cup round to his friends for them all to eat and drink. It was his third 'acted parable'. He quoted the words of his beloved Jeremiah. Nothing, for Jesus, symbolised more clearly than a supper – the meal of the day when people are relaxed, and talk and share one another's thoughts most freely – what 'God's Rule' meant. Nothing gave a clearer 'picture' of the world God is making and the way in which, in his own good time, it will really be God's world, God's family.

When the supper was over they sang a hymn. Was it those words, from one of the Hallel Hymns sung at the Passover meal, that rang in Jesus's ears as, with his friends, he stepped out into the dark street? – Or words like these from another hymn:

> Let the whole world praise God!
> Let its nations and its peoples praise him!
> How strong his love for us all is!
> We can trust him to the very end!
>
> Who is like our God
>   in heaven or earth?
> Enthroned on high,
>   watching the deep below,
> Lifting the poor and the needy
>   from the dust and the ash-heap,
> Setting them beside
>   the princes of his people!
>   Hallelujah!

Only Jesus realised how near the end was. And what an end: a slave's death on a Roman cross, executed as a threat to the Roman peace!

It was all suddenly over – 'with a loud cry and a gasp', as Mark wrote.

Or so it seemed.

Part Two

LORD AND LEADER?

New World

Bewilderment

The sudden and unexpected death of Jesus terrified his friends. It was sudden, for they do not seem to have grasped the danger Jesus was in, in spite of his own plain warnings; it was unexpected for they seem to have been convinced that God would somehow come to his help. But they had been dreaming. The brutal and terrible reality now stared them in the face: Jesus was dead and God was silent.

'He made us all feel that he was the man to set our people free,' two of his friends are reported to have said, 'but he wasn't.' That's how they felt.

All the reports show how shaken and frightened they were. They deserted Jesus in the garden. Peter, when challenged by a girl, swore that he'd never set eyes on him. They either kept to themselves in the city (with the door locked, according to the latest account) or went home. When news was brought that the tomb had been found empty, they didn't believe a word of it – they thought it a lot of humbug and nonsense.

They were not cowards; they were bewildered people whose world had fallen in ruins about them and whose nerve had broken.

We have so often been told the story of Jesus as a story full of clear and obvious signs of what we call his 'divinity' that we forget how much of this way of talking about him only happened after the event we shall be dealing with in our next chapter.

In his lifetime, as we have seen, all sorts of people, but especially his close friends, recognised that he was not just an ordinary sort of person. Exaggerated stories about him were told in the villages and at the fairs. The leaders of the Resistance Movement in Galilee were so impressed by him that they wanted him as their leader. When Jesus asked Peter what people were saying about him, Peter told him the common talk of the market place was that he was one of the great prophets – Elijah and John the Baptist were the names that came into their minds when they tried to sum him up. Peter and his friends believed he was the Chosen Leader – the 'Messiah' whom so many of his countrymen believed God would send to rescue them from foreign occupation and set them free. We have had a story about James and John who believed he would establish his 'kingdom' and wanted to get him to promise them a place in his government (see page 43). But, as Mark tells us plainly, Jesus would have none of this talk.

There was something about Jesus that commanded their loyalty and their love; but he was a puzzle. In the bottom of their hearts they did not know what to make of him. They thought of him in the conventional way they had been brought up to accept, and even held on to this way of thinking of him to the end. Then it all collapsed. Judas may have been only an extreme example of how they all thought (some of them were carrying arms when Jesus was caught in the orchard). He may have thought that Jesus, whatever he said, was the national leader sent by God to deliver his people; that Judas had only to force his hand to make him act as he ought to act to free the Jewish people and overthrow the Romans – God would give him the miraculous power to do this. So Judas betrayed him into the hands of the government – and nothing happened. Jesus accepted arrest. When Judas realised what he had done, he went out into the night and committed suicide (so the gospel of Matthew tells us).

But the point for us now to get clear is that, in his lifetime, 'there was nothing about the appearance of Jesus to demonstrate his authority . . . no outward signs to guarantee' who he was. He had been passionately concerned with one thing only – what God was doing, all he summed up in the phrase 'God's Way' ('the kingdom of God').

It was the truth about God – and about men and women and the world we live in – that Jesus tried to make clear in word and deed. He stood for something very different from popular assumptions and the religious convictions of the rabbis and the sort of thing preached in the Meeting Houses.

Indeed Jesus challenged some of the central convictions of the religion of his people, and he challenged them in no uncertain manner. He faced them in public and finally in the central shrine of the national religion, the Temple in Jerusalem. The demands he was making on both religious leaders and people were radical and revolutionary. In their eyes he was disloyal, unheroic and irreligious.

He did not mince his words either, and he did not intend to be silenced.

You have often heard, in the Meeting House, the law about murder read aloud: 'You shall not kill'. You know that a murderer will be arrested and tried before a judge. Believe me: God judges a man who is even *angry* with his brother man.

You have often heard, in the Meeting House, the law about revenge read aloud: 'An eye for an eye, a tooth for a tooth'. Believe me: there must be no fighting back – that's not the way to deal with enemies.

You have often heard, in the Meeting House, the law about fellow-citizens read aloud: 'Love your fellow-citizen'. My command is: 'Love your enemies'.

And he went further:

What bad leaders you are!
    You don't forget about the collection,
    but you forget about God's justice and his love.
    You like front seats in the Meeting House;
    and everybody touching their hats to you in the street.
    You're like gravestones that look like a pavement:
    people walk on them without knowing what's underneath.
What bad leaders you are!
    You make ordinary people carry heavy loads;
    but you don't lift a finger to help them.
    You build monuments to God's great men of old,
    but you are like your fathers who murdered them.
    You have taken away the key to the door of knowledge;
    you don't want to go in yourselves,
    and you won't let anybody else go in.

Alas for you leaders of the people:
    you clean the outside of a cup and a dish,
        but inside they are full of greed and violence.
    How blind you are!
Make the inside of the cup clean first,
    then the outside may be clean too.

A clash between Jesus and the religious authorities was not to be avoided, and when it came the government made certain what its issue would be. There was nothing to do but to get rid of him; he was a threat to all they stood for.

Jesus stood, too, for something very different from the convictions his close friends seem to have held. At that last terrible moment when he died 'with a loud cry and a gasp', the world in which they had been living, with all its hopes and dreams, suddenly became bleak and empty.

What else was there to do but to go home?

Surprise

Then – something happened.

It took them quite by surprise. When the first hints came that Jesus's death may not have been the end, it struck his friends, on their own confession, as 'humbug and nonsense'.

After all, death is death.

And such a death!

Hanging on a cross was the ultimate penalty for murderers, robbers, mischief-makers, and it was the typical punishment for slaves. Crucifixion was a horrible and cruel death – 'it included flogging beforehand, the victim often carried the beam to the place of execution, where he was nailed to it with outstretched arms, raised up and seated on a wooden peg'. Slaves and foreigners in the Roman Empire knew that such a punishment, whether by government authorities or even landlords, might well one day be their fate. When Jesus talked about being ready to 'take up your cross' this was the death he was thinking of.

For Jewish people such a death had an added horror – it had a religious meaning. The Jewish Law was quite clear about it:

If a man has committed a crime punishable by death and he is put to death, and you hang him on a tree, his body shall not remain all night upon the tree, but you shall bury him the same day, for a hanged man is accursed by God; you shall not defile your land which the Lord your God gives you for an inheritance.

How, then, could such a death be other than final?

But something had happened beyond anything they could have imagined and outside anything they could have thought possible. They suddenly realised that Jesus's death was not the end but the beginning and it took their breath away. They were filled with surprise, and fear, and joy.

We have several reports of what happened – in the gospels and in Paul's letters – and we must sort them out. Whatever happened, it changed the whole way his friends lived and felt and thought. As Paul put it, 'the old world has gone and a new world has been born'.

Three quotations from Paul's letters (he was writing about A.D. 55) will be enough to show us what a change had taken place in the lives of Jesus's friends:

We've finished with the old ways of living with all their nasty tricks. We're living in a new world – God's world – and every day God will make us better at living in it.

You've heard people talking like this, haven't you? – 'My country – right or wrong', 'We're civilised; they're wogs', 'Some people are born slaves; they'll always be slaves'. We don't talk like that any more.

We stand – always and everywhere – for all that Jesus stood for.

Jesus has broken down all barriers. He is all that matters, and he is changing the whole life of mankind.

The love of Jesus drives us on – when we realise that he gave his life for all mankind, so that everybody should have something bigger to live for than just himself and what he can get for himself. Jesus gave his life for everybody.

We don't think of people now in the way people ordinarily think of one another. (I once thought of Jesus as my enemy and the enemy of my people. I don't think of him like that any more.) We try to think of people as God thinks of them.

When anybody becomes a friend of Jesus, the world's a new world for him; the old world has gone and a new world has been born.

But we know now that the world is not the sort of world we once thought it was. It is a world where God works for all that is worthwhile, *alongside those who love him*. We are fellow-workers with God. This is what he was always calling us to be – with one purpose in mind, a purpose he planned and settled before history began. This purpose was that we might grow up to be the kind of person Jesus was; so that Jesus might be the elder brother of a great family of brothers and sisters.

Paul is only saying what all the early friends of Jesus would have said; it was not just the memory of Jesus that had changed them; God had vindicated Jesus in an unmistakable manner – he was still a real presence with them.

What, then, had happened?

Here are Paul's own words:

I handed on to you, as the central fact of our Christian faith, the account I was given. . . . 'He died and was buried. On the third day he was raised to life. He was seen by Peter; then by "The Twelve". After that, he was seen by more than five hundred at once; most of them are still living, but some have since died. He was then seen by James, his brother; then by all his close friends.'

Paul then added some words about himself: 'Last of all, long after anybody could have hoped, he was seen by me also'.

Two things must be noted here.

First of all, Paul is writing to Christian friends who even some twenty years after the execution of Jesus are finding it difficult to understand what 'the resurrection from the dead' means. Whatever happened was always difficult to describe or explain.

Secondly, Paul is not just writing what he himself thought about it. He tells us he is reporting what was 'handed on' to him, probably at his baptism within a year or two of the event he is reporting. This was the authoritative account given from the beginning.

Paul also says, as we have seen, that his own experience was like those of Peter and the others. His own description of this experience is quite brief. He writes in another of his letters that what happened to him was that God 'chose to reveal his Son to me'.

This is our earliest evidence that something very unexpected had happened. We will come back in another chapter to look more closely at what this new experience meant. But it is important now to remember that this new experience was open and public and demands some kind of explanation.

This brings us back to what happened 'on the third day' – the day that was referred to in the 'most important' statement given to Paul at his baptism. Paul himself simply says 'On the third day he was raised to life'.

What actually happened then?

There were circulating among the Christian communities various accounts of how on the 'third day' (our 'Easter Sunday') the tomb was found empty. No description of the resurrection of Jesus itself was ever attempted; only his 'appearances' are described. The accounts differ very much among themselves on many matters – who was the first to 'see' Jesus, what the women did when they got to the tomb, where the appearances of Jesus took place – in Jerusalem or in Galilee. But all agree that the tomb was found empty. Mark's account runs like this:

When the Holy Day of the Jews was over, three women friends of Jesus – Mary of Magdala, Mary who was James's mother, and Salome – brought sweet-smelling oils to anoint his body.

They got to his grave very early on Sunday, just as the sun was rising.

'Who will roll the stone away from the cave's mouth for us?' they said to one another.

It was a very big stone. They looked up and saw that it had already been rolled away.

They went into the cave and they were amazed to see a young man in white clothes sitting on the right-hand side.

'Don't be frightened,' he said. 'You are looking for Jesus of Nazareth who was put to death. He has risen. You won't find him here; you can see where they put his body. Go and tell his friends that he will be in Galilee before you and you will see him there, as he told you. And don't forget Peter.'

They ran out of the cave trembling with terror. They were so frightened that they didn't say a word to anyone.

It is important for us to remember, however, that it was not the empty tomb that convinced his friends that Jesus had been 'raised from death' but the new experience of God which Jesus made possible. What they believed God had done was the ground of their conviction. Their new experience of God was tied up with Jesus – his life in Galilee, his dreadful death and what they called his 'appearances' after his death.

The empty tomb, moreover, doesn't *prove* anything. Many explanations could quite reasonably be given – that his friends had stolen his body; that the women went to the wrong tomb (in the rush and confusion it might so happen); that somebody had removed the body (as Mary of Magdala, the Fourth Gospel reports, thought the gardener had done). It looks, however, as if the first friends of Jesus had in their hands an early report which they did not know what to do with, and there is no reason for us to doubt that women friends of Jesus found the tomb empty (as a Jewish scholar says is clear) and that they were certain it was the tomb in which Jesus had been buried.

But the convincing evidence, as Paul saw, was this new experience of God which changed the whole way in which the friends of Jesus lived and thought, and which made them 'new men'. Here is Paul's description of the new experience; it comes from the letter he wrote to the Roman Christians (see *New World* pp.252ff.–295ff. in 1st edn.).

Looking back on all this, what shall we say?

If God is standing by us, what does it matter who opposes us? He did not spare his own Son; he gave him up for us all. With such a gift, will he not give us everything else as well?

Who can take God's love away from us now – the love which Jesus had made real to us?

You know the sort of thing that can happen to any of us in this world of ours – suffering, hardship, cruelty, hunger, homelessness, danger, war. In just such a world, we who are the friends of Jesus can live more splendidly than the greatest world-conquerors – with the help of Jesus who loved us.

I am quite sure that nothing – neither dying nor living, neither what we're facing now nor what we may have to face tomorrow, nothing in our own world or in outer space or in our own hearts, can take away from us God's love, made real by Jesus our Lord.

We must look a little more closely at what this new experience of God meant to the friends of Jesus.

New job : 'to the ends of the earth'

The new experience of God, for the friends of Jesus, meant new convictions and a new job.

When something big and dramatic happens to us – something which stops us in our tracks, makes us think about everything in a different way and perhaps changes the very direction in which we were going – it takes us a long time to grasp what it means. We have to do more than think about it; we have to do something about it. It's in doing something about it that we really get our thinking straight.

The friends of Jesus took a long time to get their thinking straight. But it was in doing something about what he meant to them that they began to clear their minds about what Jesus stood for.

There were three steps that their new experience of God compelled them to take. First, they found that they had got a new job on their hands: they had been given good news, not just for their own people, but for the whole world, everybody everywhere, and they must carry it across all frontiers of race or class or creed.

Secondly, in tackling this job – and some of them tackled it rather unwillingly, it went against the grain – they were given a new vision of God and of themselves and of the world they were living in.

Thirdly, this new vision made them begin to rethink everything in a way very different from the conventional, traditional ways in which they had been brought up.

We begin with their new job.

It is worth noting that they found themselves in a world where, perhaps for the first time, a *world* vision and a *world* job could mean something to ordinary men and women – to fishermen and builders and tent-makers, the kind of people most of the friends of Jesus were. The Roman Peace gave freedom of travel on land and sea across the known world, and the Greek language, the common language of that world, gave the small group of men whom Jesus had gathered round him the very tools they would need.

Here is a story about Peter. Luke, in his account of Jesus and his friends (in the two volumes about them: volume one, his *Gospel* and volume two, *The Acts*) thought this a most important story, and so told it at length. It was a story of the first foreigner to become a Christian – the most unlikely of persons, an officer in the Roman army. It was also a story of how slow and reluctant Peter, of all people, was, and how he remembered something Jesus once said.

Caesarea was the headquarters of the Roman Army in Palestine, and among the officers there was a man called Cornelius, a captain of the Italian Regiment. He was a good man who, with all his family, loved God. He was always ready to help anybody in need and prayed to God every day.

One day, about three o'clock in the afternoon, he had a dream. Everything was very clear and he saw an angel of God coming towards him.

'Cornelius,' the angel called.

He stared at his visitor in terror.

'What's the matter, sir?' he asked.

'God knows all about you, your prayers and your good deeds,' he said. 'Send to Joppa and fetch a man called Simon – he's also known as Peter. He is staying with Simon the tanner; his house faces the sea.'

The angel left him.

Cornelius, without wasting a minute, called two of his slaves and one of his soldiers who loved God as he did, told them all about his dream and sent them off to Joppa.

About noon next day, the three men were well on their way and had almost reached Joppa.

It was about noon that Peter went up on to the flat roof of the house to pray. He suddenly felt hungry and wanted his dinner, but while the servants were getting it ready he fell asleep and started to dream.

It was a strange dream.

He saw something dropping down out of the open sky – something like a great sheet, tied at the four corners and being lowered to the earth. All sorts of animals and reptiles and wild birds were inside, including things no Jew, by Jewish law, was allowed to eat.

He heard a Voice speaking.

'Get up, Peter,' it said, 'kill and eat them.'

'Never, sir,' said Peter. 'I've never eaten any forbidden food.'

'What God calls good food,' said the Voice, 'you mustn't call forbidden food.'

This happened three times. Then the thing was suddenly drawn up into the sky.

While Peter was wondering what the dream could mean, the messengers of Cornelius stood outside the gate; all this time they had been asking people the way to Simon's house.

'Is Simon, called Peter, staying here?' they called out.

Peter was still up on the roof, wondering about the dream.

'There are three men looking for you,' God told him. 'Get up and go down to them and go along with them. There's nothing to worry about; I've sent them.'

Peter went down to the men.

'I am the man you are looking for,' he said. 'What have you come for?'

'We come from Captain Cornelius, a good man who loves God – all the Jews in Caesarea will tell you that. He was told by God to invite you to his house, and to listen to what you have to say.'

Peter asked them to stay with him. Next morning, he got up and went off with them. Some of the Christians in Joppa went along with him.

They got to Caesarea the next day.

Captain Cornelius had asked his relatives and close friends to come along, and was looking out for Peter and the three men. He met Peter as he was entering the house, and fell down on the ground in front of him; he thought Peter must be no ordinary man.

Peter pulled him to his feet.

'Stand up,' he said, 'I'm an ordinary man like yourself.'

Talking with Cornelius, he went on into the crowded house.

'You all know about Jewish Law,' he said. 'You know it forbids a Jew to have anything to do with a foreigner – even to visit him. But I now know better, for God has made it quite clear to me that I must not call anybody at all, whoever he is, "foreigner". I couldn't say No when you sent for me. Tell me why you wanted me to come.'

Captain Cornelius told him about his dream.

'So, you see,' he said, 'I sent at once to invite you and you have kindly come along. All of us in this room know God is here, and we want to listen to what God has told you to tell us.'

'It's as clear as daylight to me now,' said Peter, 'that God has no favourites. It doesn't matter what race or nation you belong to; if you love God and do what is right, God welcomes you.

'You know what the Bible says –

> He sent his word and healed them.

and

> How lovely on the hills
>   are the footsteps of the man who brings the Good News
>   and calls all the world to be at peace.

'All this is really about Jesus.

'He is God's Chosen Leader; all the world is his Kingdom, and he has brought the Good News of peace.

'You yourselves, too, know something about what has happened in Palestine in our own time – the events that began in Galilee after John the Baptist had been preaching in Jordan Valley, and the story of Jesus from Nazareth.

'Let me tell you what really happened.

'God called Jesus to his great work, and gave him his Spirit and power. He went from village to village doing good and healing sick people; for God was with him. We saw with our own eyes all he did in Palestine and in Jerusalem City.

'He died on a Roman cross; but God soon raised him from the dead – the same Jesus we had known in Galilee. The crowds didn't see him; only those whom God had chosen saw him – we who had supper with him when he was alive again. He told us what to do: to tell the Good News to everybody, and to make it quite clear that, in all he said and did, God has shown us what is right and what is wrong. Jesus, not Caesar or Moses, is the judge of all men everywhere. Everybody who trusts in Jesus is forgiven for all the wrong things he has done – because he was what he was. This is surely what the Bible tells us.'

Peter was still speaking when God's power was given to everybody who had been listening to him. The Jewish Christians who had come along with Peter were amazed – fancy God giving his power even to *foreigners*! They themselves heard them, there in the room, singing God's praises!

'God has given his power to these foreigners just as he gave it to us Jews,' said Peter. 'Can anybody say they ought not to join the company of the Christians?'

He gave orders for them to be baptised 'in the name of Jesus'.

Whatever hesitations Peter had – and we shall see that he had a real struggle with himself – it was Paul who saw most clearly what Jesus lived and died for. Even he didn't see it all at once; it took him many years to grasp what (to use his own words) the love of Jesus was driving him to do. When he did grasp it, he found himself a traveller across the world and often in great danger:

Let me tell you what I've had to face. I know it's silly for me to talk like this, but here's the list. I know what it is to work hard and live dangerously.

I've been beaten up more times than I can remember, been in more than one prison, and faced death itself more than once. Five times I've been thrashed by a Jewish court to within an inch of my life; three times I've been beaten with rods by city magistrates; and once I was nearly stoned to death.

I've been shipwrecked three times; and once, I was adrift, out of sight of land, for twenty-four hours.

I don't know how many roads I've tramped. I've faced bandits; I've been attacked by fellow-countrymen and by foreigners. I've met danger in city streets and on lonely country roads and out in the open sea.

Here are two typical stories. In the first, Paul found himself facing people in remote highlands with their strange language and strange religion. In the second, he found himself debating with learned teachers in the most famous city of all, Athens:

Barnabas and Paul came one day to the old town of Lystra, high up in the highlands of Anatolia, where people, though they could speak Greek, usually spoke their own strange language which Paul and Barnabas couldn't understand.

There was a man here who had been a cripple all his life and had never been able to walk.

Paul was talking to the crowd near the town gates and the cripple sat there on the roadside listening to him. Paul looked straight at him and saw that the man believed he could cure him.

'Get up on your feet!' said Paul, loudly enough for everybody to hear. 'Stand up straight!'

The cripple jumped up and walked about.

The crowd saw what Paul had done, and they started shouting in their own strange language.

'The gods have come down like men and are here in our city!' they said.

They thought Barnabas was the great god Zeus, and Paul the messenger of the gods, Hermes – because he did all the talking!

The priest of Zeus, who looked after the nearby temple called 'The Temple of Zeus-outside-the-Town', brought bulls wreathed with flowers to the town gates, to sacrifice to Barnabas and Paul as gods.

Barnabas and Paul couldn't help but hear all this noise. When they saw what it all meant, they tore their clothes and ran among the crowd.

'Sirs!' they shouted. 'What's all this for? We are just ordinary men like you, and all we're doing is bringing you good news. Stop all this nonsense and learn what God is really like. He's the living God; he made the sky and land and seas. He made the whole world. Until now God let people everywhere do what they thought best. Yet even then he showed you what he was like. He looked after you all. He gave you rain from the sky and harvest time. He saw that you had food to eat. All your happiness comes from him.'

Even words like this hardly stopped the crowd from going on with their sacrifice.

Then Jews from the towns where Paul and Barnabas had already been

came along and told the crowd what *they* thought about them. That turned the crowd against them, and they started throwing stones at Paul. They thought they had killed him, and dragged him outside the town.

Paul's friends stood round him; they, too, thought he was dead. But he got up and went back into the town.

Paul came to Athens by boat, and he was waiting there for Silas and Timothy.

He wandered through the streets; everywhere there were temples and images of the Greek gods. This made Paul very unhappy. He had to talk to somebody about it. He went to the Jewish Meeting House and argued there; he went to the market place and argued with anybody who happened to be there. There were many lecturers in the city, for its university was very famous; some of them met Paul, and he argued with them.

'What's this chatterer talking about?' sneered some.

'It's some foreign fellow talking about his gods, it seems,' said others.

The City Council was called 'Mars Hill', after the name of the hill where

it used to meet in earlier times. This Council was specially interested in all
new speakers who came to teach in Athens. The citizens of Athens and their
foreign visitors always had time to talk about or listen to anything strange
and new; they seemed to do nothing else.

The lecturers got hold of Paul and took him before the Council.

'Tell us, if you please, something more about this "news" of yours,' they
said. 'What you've been talking about sounds very strange to us. We'd like
to know what it's all about.'

Paul stood before the Council.

'Citizens of Athens,' he said, 'by just wandering around your streets, I
can see that religion matters very much to you. I had a good look at your
temples and the images of your gods. And I noticed one altar that had these
words on it "To an Unknown God". You do not know him; I will tell you
about him.

'The God who made the world and all that's in it by that very fact is the
Master of the whole world. His home can't be a temple in a street that you

can build with your own hands. He can't need temple servants, as though he had to have somebody looking after him. He gave us the very lives we live and everything we have. We may belong to different nations now, but at the beginning God made us all one people and gave us the whole world for our home. All things are in his hands – the rise and fall of nations and the boundaries of their territories. He did all this for one purpose only – the men and women might look for him and find him.

'Yet he is very near every one of us. Your own poets have said this very thing –

In God we live and move and exist,

and

We, too, belong to his family.

'If, therefore, we belong to God, we can't possibly think that gold and silver and stone are good enough to show us what he is like. No artist can paint God's picture, however clever or thoughtful he may be.

'What, then, has God done? He takes no notice of the past, when we didn't know what he is like. But today, in our own time, he calls all people to change their ways. We can no longer say we do not know; Jesus has made him plain. The day is fixed when everybody everywhere will be judged by this man he has chosen – and truly judged. The proof of this he has given to all men – he has raised him from the dead.'

Some of them laughed out loud at Paul when they heard him talk like this – about God 'raising Jesus from the dead'. But there were others.

'We'll hear you again about all this,' they said.

What the new experience of God made clear to most of the friends of Jesus – but not to all of them – was that God's love, which Jesus made real to them, was for the whole world – everybody, everywhere.

Men come slowly to great convictions. There was a heart-searching debate among the early Christians: did Jesus come to reform the Jewish religion? Or did he come to call everybody everywhere to become God's family, each in his own way?

Even Peter still hesitated to go the whole way; and once in the city of Antioch Paul faced him on this issue. He described what happened in a letter:

Our difficulties in getting the Good News clear were by no means over. This is the sort of thing that happened.

Barnabas and I, some time later, were back in Antioch, and Peter joined us there. But I had to stand up to him and tell him that he was plainly in the wrong – on this same question.

When he first came there, he ate his meals with all of us; foreigner and Jew sat down together at the same table. Then some men came from Jerusalem (they said that James had sent them), and everything changed. He started to stay away from our common meals. He was frightened of these Jewish Christians who said that you couldn't become a Christian if you hadn't first become a proper Jew. Other friends of Jesus in Antioch started to do the same – even Barnabas was deceived.

This was cheating – and cheating about the very thing that makes the Good News really good news. It was as plain as plain could be to me.

One day, when everybody was together, I tackled Peter.

'When you first came here,' I said, 'born and bred a Jew though you are, you "lived like a foreigner, not like a Jew", as these men put it. Why have you turned round, and now try to make foreigners "live like Jews"?'

I went on to put the Good News plainly. I myself am a Jew by race and not a foreigner. But I know that a man doesn't become a Christian by carrying out all the details of the Jewish religion. He becomes a Christian by just trusting Jesus himself. That is the heart of the matter.

I know what is the secret of my own life. I go on living my ordinary life it is true, and yet, in a sense, I don't feel *I'm* living it – Jesus has taken charge of me. I live by trusting Jesus, God's Son, who loved me and gave his life for me.

What, then, was the vision that became clearer and clearer as foreigners, to the great surprise of some of the Palestinian Christians, became Christians too?

New experience: 'the light shining from the face of Jesus'

It was, as we have seen, out in the world beyond Palestine that what Jesus meant – why he lived as he did, how he died, how he was 'raised to life' – became clearer. It meant nothing less than the vision of a new world, God's world, and a call to be God's 'fellow-workers' in its making. Nothing could have made this vision sharper than the sight of men and women, of different races and classes and nations, becoming Christians. Their old fears vanished; a new joy marked their lives.

When Paul tried to describe what a difference Jesus had made to him he went back to the opening words of the book of Genesis and the story of the making of the world as the only kind of language he could use:

God, who made this bright world, filled my heart with light, the light which shines when we know him as he is, the light shining from the face of Jesus.

This is Paul's account of his own experience; but it was, as he was constantly saying, an experience in which everybody everywhere could share. Here he is writing to those who had become Christians in the highlands of Anatolia:

Your trust in God your Father has made you members of his Family; Jesus has made this possible. For when you were baptised and became Christians, you began, with his help, to live in his way – as he lived in his Father's Way.

Living in God's Way means that you can't talk about one another as being 'white' or 'coloured', 'working-class' or 'upper-class', 'men' or 'women' – as though that was the only thing about them that matters. The most important thing is that as Christians you are one company of friends. And if you are friends of Jesus, you are members of God's Family as God meant you to be and promised to make you.

That is why, when the time was ripe, God sent his Son to live among us as one of us – to help us to live as his sons and daughters, grown-up members of his Family. Because this is what we now are, he has given us the spirit of his Son in our hearts. When we pray to him, we pray as Jesus did; we say 'Father!'

You aren't God's slaves; God has made you, as I have said, his sons and daughters. And, as sons and daughters inherit their father's wealth, so all the wealth of God, your Father, is yours.

Note how Paul, when he is describing this new experience, has to go back to the story of Jesus, remembering how he lived and how he died. For Paul it was the way Jesus died which made real what God's love was like – a love which, in his own words, was 'broad and long and high and deep'; and it was the way God had raised him from the dead that showed us how great the power of God's love is.

The very word 'cross' sounded differently. To any Roman citizen it could only sound a savage word – like our 'gallows' or 'firing-squad'. It was the way Romans executed foreign criminals or rebels or slaves. But now it was for Paul the symbol of God's 'amazing love' – he even wrote once to some friends that he could 'boast' about it.

What Jesus had made plain for Paul was that God was someone we could trust and to whom we could pray as 'Father' (here Paul used the very word that Jesus used in his own prayers – 'Abba'). There is nothing we need fear – not even death itself, for death (as Paul once said – he was quoting) 'has been totally defeated'. The whole world – this world and whatever may lie beyond it – is God our Father's world.

To many people today the word 'resurrection' is meaningless. They find the idea of resurrection not only difficult but incredible. We need to remember that it never was easy or credible – that's why Jesus's friends were taken by surprise. For Jewish people the whole story of an executed criminal who was raised by God to life was a 'stumbling block', an obstacle that prevented them from taking the story of Jesus seriously. For educated people in the world outside Palestine it was just 'rubbish'. Some Christians found that they couldn't understand what it meant.

Here is how Paul tried to explain it:

The heart of the Good News is that Jesus is not dead but alive. How, then, can some people say, 'There's no such thing as being raised from death'? If that is so, Jesus never conquered death; and if Jesus never conquered death, there is no Good News to tell, and we've been living in a fool's paradise. We've even been telling lies about God, when we said he raised Jesus from death; for he didn't – if 'there's no such thing as being raised from death'. And if 'there's no such thing as being raised from death', Jesus is just – dead. If Jesus is dead and has not been raised to life again, all we've lived for as friends of Jesus is just an empty dream, and we're just where we were, help-less to do anything about the evil in our hearts and in the world. And those who have died as friends of Jesus have now found out the bitter truth. If all we've got is a *story* about Jesus inspiring us just to live this life better, we of all men are most to be pitied.

Of course, the whole idea of 'being raised from death' raises many ques-tions for many people. For example – 'How are dead people raised to life?' 'What sort of body do they have then?' But questions like these sound silly when we remember what kind of world God's world is and what God him-self is like. Take the seed the farmer sows – it must die before it can grow. The seed he sows is only bare grain; it is nothing like the plant he'll see at harvest-time. This is the way God has created the world of nature; every kind of seed grows up into its own kind of plant – its new body. This is true of the world of animals, too, where there is a great variety of life, men, animals, birds, fish – all different from one another.

This shows us how to think about this matter of 'being raised from death'. There's the life men live on earth – that has its own splendour; and there's the life men live when they are 'raised from death' and live (as we say) 'in heaven' – and this world beyond our earthly world has its own different splendour.

The splendour of the sun and the splendour of the moon and the splendour of the stars differ from one another – even the stars differ in splendour.

So it is when men are 'raised from death'. Here the body is a 'physical' body; there it is raised a 'spiritual' body. Here everything grows old and decays; there it is raised in a form which neither grows old nor decays. Here the human body can suffer shame and shock; there it is raised in splendour. Here it is weak; there it is full of vigour.

This is the meaning of the words of the Bible – 'Death has been totally defeated'.

For the fact is Jesus *was* raised to life. God be thanked – we can now live victoriously because of what he has done.

So, for the early Christians, it was God our Father's world in spite of all that could happen in it – 'suffering, hardship, cruelty, hunger, homelessness, danger, war' (the list is Paul's). In a real sense, it was a world in the making, and what Jesus had made clear is that they were called to be God's 'fellow-workers' in its making. And so (to put it now in our own words), if we accept the story of Jesus, we suddenly become aware of who we are and what our job is. We take our place in the world's work with everybody else – as engineers, teachers, shopkeepers, shorthand typists, farmers, nurses, doctors, managers, shop-stewards. But we are not just engineers, teachers, shopkeepers, shorthand typists, farmers, nurses, doctors, managers, shop-stewards. We are members of God's Family and God's fellow-workers. We look with new eyes at the world around us – the village or town or city where we live and our place in it – and at the world we read about in the newspapers (not only at what is reported there, but at all the important things that never get reported). And it is not just what happens in this world that matters. Death itself has been totally defeated – this world is but an exciting beginning.

How, then, do we begin? Again, two quotations from Paul's letters will show how his first friends felt:

Love must be *sincere and straightforward.* Have nothing to do with evil of any kind. *Give your heart to everything that is good.*

Be a real family, warm-hearted in your care of one another, thinking better of others than of yourselves.

When keenness is called for, let's have no laziness; on fire with the spirit of Jesus, give yourselves to his service.

Look forward to God's new world with gladness. In hard times stand your ground; *never forget to pray.*

Take your part in helping other friends of Jesus when they are in want; make it your aim to keep the doors of your home open to those who need it.

Remember the words of Jesus: '*Bless those who treat you badly; bless them – don't curse them.*'

Share other people's happiness and other people's sadness. Learn to respect everybody.

Don't be proud. *Mix with ordinary people.*

Don't talk as if you knew all the answers.

Don't injure anybody just because he has injured you; do the right thing that all men, in their hearts, know is right.

As far as you can, be friends with everybody. Never try to get your own back, my friends; leave that in God's hands. You know what the Bible says: ' "I will see justice done," says God: "punishment is in my hands." '

Remember what the Bible also says:

> If your enemy is hungry
> > give him food;
> if he is thirsty,
> > give him drink.
> If you do this,
> > you will make him ashamed of himself.

Don't be beaten by evil; beat evil by doing good.

Remember who you are: God has chosen you, you belong to him and he loves you. His way must be your way.

Care for people. Be kind and gentle and never think about yourself. Stand up to everything. Put up with people's wounding ways; when you have real cause to complain, don't – forgive them.

Here is your clue: God's forgiveness of you is the measure of the forgiveness you must show to others.

It is love like the love of Jesus that makes all these things possible, holding everything in its grip and never stopping half way. Master every situation with the quietness of heart which Jesus gives us. This is how you were meant to live; not each by himself, but together in company with all the friends of Jesus. Thank God that it is so.

Remember Jesus, and keep the Good News, with all its wealth of meaning, day by day in your mind. Here is real wisdom, in the light of which you can help one another, deepening one another's understanding and warning one another, if need be.

How full of songs your hearts will be, songs of joy and praise and love, songs to God himself! In this spirit you can take everything in your stride, matching word and deed, as the friends of the Lord Jesus. Make him the centre of your life; and with his help let your hearts be filled with thankfulness to God – your Father.

In the first quotation I have printed in italics words of Jesus that Paul was either quoting or echoing. In the second quotation, too, it is clear how the example of Jesus guided him in his thinking about Christian behaviour.

So it all came back to Jesus. Their new experience of God made his friends talk about him in a very strange way. He was not just a dead leader. Who, then, was he?

New convictions: 'The Lord Jesus Christ'

The first Christians were in a dilemma. They were Jews. They held in contempt the many and strange 'gods' worshipped in foreign countries. Their faith was clear:

> Listen, O people!
> There is one God only;
> you must love God with everything you are –
> your heart, your soul, your body.

Nothing was more certain than that.

Yet now they found that they could not think about God without thinking about Jesus; and they could not think about Jesus without thinking about God. Jesus had not spoken about himself. Who was he? They began by talking about him as 'God's Servant'.

One thing all his friends were certain about: God was behind the whole story of Jesus. 'In Jesus,' wrote Paul, 'God is making everybody everywhere his friends.' This was not something sudden on God's part, as though he had dramatically intervened in our human story. It was part of his whole purpose in creating the world: that we 'might grow up to be the kind of person Jesus was, so that Jesus might be the elder brother of a great family of brothers and sisters'. The new experience of his love and power was also part of his plan. And it was all tied up with the story of Jesus. So Paul can talk about 'living in Christ', or 'Christ in us', or 'having the spirit of Christ', or 'having God's spirit living in us', or 'being led by God's spirit'.

We find the early Christians using all sorts of words to describe him, for, however they thought of what God was doing in the world, Jesus was at the centre of it. He was the clue by which they had begun to understand and make sense of the world in which they were living and the strange and tragic story of human history. We have already used one of the words they used to describe who Jesus was – 'Christ'.

Let us sort a few of them out.

Two of the words may go back to Jesus himself.

One we have already noted – 'servant'. This is an old word, used in the Old Testament to describe high officers of state (they are the 'King's Servants'); and to describe the men of God we call the prophets (they are 'God's Servants'). There are some famous old poems which describe the Hebrew people themselves as 'God's Servant'.

The other word which probably goes back to Jesus himself is 'Son of Man' which sounds strange in English; it sounded strange in Greek too. It was the Hebrew and Aramaic way of saying 'man' and it could even be used, too, to describe, as the word 'servant' did, the Jewish people themselves who believed themselves to be 'God's People'. If Jesus did use these words to describe his work, he was speaking, it seems, not just about himself but about himself and his friends, the new 'People of God'.

The word 'Christ' (the Greek translation of 'Messiah' – meaning 'the one who is anointed') was a word Jesus did not like. We have seen that when Peter used the word of him, he rebuked him for doing so. But it was a word with a long history. Kings had been 'anointed'; and prophets had been spoken of as 'anointed'. The word was once used of a foreign emperor, Cyrus. In the years before Jesus, the word had come to represent God's 'Chosen Leader' whom the Jewish people expected God to send as their deliverer. But this 'Chosen Leader' was thought of in many different ways – sometimes as a supernatural figure, sometimes as a soldier. Yet although Jesus did not like the word and did not use it of himself, Pilate executed him as a 'messiah', a claimant to the leadership of the Jewish people – 'the Jewish King', as he put it on the official death-notice on the cross.

It seemed to Jewish Christians that (in spite of his dislike of the word) no word described him better – he *was* 'God's Chosen Leader'. They began to talk about him as 'Jesus the Messiah', where 'Messiah' is a simple descriptive name. When 'Messiah', however, was translated into Greek as 'Christ', it began to change its meaning. Greek-speaking foreigners didn't understand it. They simply used it as Jesus's second name.

Paul used the word 'Christ' to describe the whole influence of Jesus – his life in Palestine and the new experience of God which he made possible, so that he could use the words 'Spirit', 'Spirit of God' and 'Spirit of Christ', as we have seen, to describe the new experience of God Jesus made possible. Paul was struggling with an almost impossible task, and he was aware how difficult it was. But to talk about Jesus as though he was just a good man who had died was to be false to what he felt in his heart the new experience of God to be; he was for him much more than that. But how do you describe that 'much more'?

Another word the Christians used was 'Lord'. This became the common description of Jesus; he was 'the Lord Jesus Christ'. The word 'Lord' had been used for God in the Old Testament; God was 'Lord'. It was also used to describe the Roman Emperors and some of the foreign gods ('There are many gods and many lords', Paul once wrote). So it came to be used of Jesus; to say that 'Jesus is Lord' became the simplest way of describing Christian faith.

It was the new experience of God – the sense of his presence, of his love and his forgiveness, of the power to live in his way, which he gave to all who accepted his love – which lay at the back of this struggle to find words that really described what Jesus meant. So we find two of the first Christians talking like this about their new convictions:

God is love itself. So, if we live in love – and we can see what this means by remembering how Jesus lived – we live in God's presence and he lives in our hearts. With love like this in our hearts – the love for God and love for one another – there's nothing that can ever make us afraid, for such love drives all fear away.

You see, God loved us first, and we learned how to love from him.

God has shown us clearly what he is like in a new way – how he stands for what is right, overthrows what is wrong and helps men to live in his Way.

This is not altogether a new Way, as we have seen – the Men of God of the Jewish people had begun to see how God puts wrongs right. But Jesus has made it quite plain. If we are to live in God's Way, we must trust God; this means trusting in Jesus who has made God real to us.

This is true for everybody everywhere; for God, as we have seen, has no favourites. We have all done wrong; none of us has lived as splendidly as God intended him to live, though we were all created to live in his Way and be like him. But God treats us as if we had learned to live splendidly; his love is given to us freely. And it is Jesus who has won this freedom for us.

There is nothing in all this to make us proud of ourselves. Keeping all the rules wouldn't have stopped us being proud of ourselves. We have simply taken him at his word, and that leaves no room for boasting.

I am sure of this: everybody can really live as God wants him to live by simply trusting him, not by trying to keep all the rules. I mean everybody. Is God only the God of the Jewish people? Isn't he the God of all people everywhere? Of course he is, for there is only one God. So he puts Jewish people right – if they trust him; and he puts the people of other countries right if they trust him.

The stories of Jesus's birth, with which Matthew and Luke begin their accounts of him, are setting out, as great prefaces to his story, the convictions which his first friends held about him. As we now have them, they are a mixture of history and symbolism and poetry. We really know very little about Jesus's birth and early life. Luke mentions his boyhood but he gives us only one story – the story of his visit to Jerusalem as a boy.

Jesus appears suddenly when at about the age of thirty he went south to join John the Baptist's movement. The simple and beautiful stories of his birth, using legendary material (about wandering eastern astrologers, moving stars, angelic choirs) and quotations from the Old Testament prophets and hymn-writers, celebrate in picture language the conviction that Jesus fulfilled the hopes of both Jews and foreigners and that God was speaking to the whole world in him.

The most famous attempt to describe all that Jesus means are the words – a poem – which open the latest account of Jesus in the New Testament, *The Gospel of John*. A well-known Greek word for 'word' or 'reason' or 'wisdom' is used to describe Jesus – he is God's 'word' to the world, God's 'reason', God's 'wisdom'. The poem begins with words that echo the opening words of the book of Genesis which Paul, we remember, once used to describe his new experience of God 'in Christ':

> At the beginning of all things –
> 'the Word.
> God and the Word,
> God himself.
>
> At the beginning of all things,
> the Word and God.
>
> All things became what they are
> through the Word;
> without the Word
> nothing ever became anything.
>
> It was the Word
> that made everything alive;
> and it was this 'being alive'
> that has been the Light by which men have found their way.
> The Light is still shining in the Darkness;
> The Darkness has never put it out.

The real Light
    shining on every man alive
        was dawning.
It was dawning on the world of men,
    it was what made the world a real world,
        but nobody recognised it.

The whole world was its true home,
    yet men, crown of creation, turned their backs on it.
But to those who walked by this Light,
    to those who trusted it,
it gave the right to become
    members of God's Family.

These became what they were –
    not because 'they were born like that',
    not because 'it's human nature to live like that',
    not because men 'chose to live like that' –
but because God himself gave them their new life.

The Word became human
    and lived a human life like ours.
We saw his splendour,
    love's splendour, real splendour.

From the richness of his life,
    all of us have received endless kindness:
God showed us what his service meant through Moses;
    he made his love real to us through Jesus.

Nobody has ever seen God himself;
    the beloved Son,
    who knows his Father's secret thoughts,
        has made him plain.

Personal Epilogue

I had intended to end this book with a brief chapter on what Jesus has meant to people – people within his community and outside it, people of different centuries and races and countries. That's a story worth telling – and an important one if we are to come to grips with his meaning. But, as I came near the end of my account of him, I began to feel that that was not what I ought to do. I ought just to say simply something of what he means to me. I tried to find some excuse for dodging this. But, now I come to the end, I know that, for me, that is what I must do.

I do it for two reasons. The first is that the story of Jesus is not, for me, just a story of something that happened a long time ago. I doubt whether I would have written this book at all if that is what the story had meant to me – a fine story but an old one. I have never all my life been able to get out of the haunting conviction that somehow this is a story I have got to live with. And it has indeed, in however inadequate a fashion, been a decisive story for me, and introduced me to places and people I don't think I would otherwise have ever known – to north-west China and to the east end of Sheffield, for example. If I ask myself why, I hardly know what to say, except that in this story of Jesus I felt that I had been given the clue to what this world's about and the sort of thing I ought to be doing in it.

The second reason is this. The story of Jesus, as I have tried to set it out, is there for you, the reader, to explore for yourself and to make up your own mind about. It is not for me or anybody else to tell you what to think. But it will be already clear that I think the story of Jesus is a critical and vital one for the whole future of humanity. I hold this as a plain matter of fact and quite apart from the great claims that Christians have made for him. If you think I'm wrong, you won't bother with this story any further. If you think I'm on the right track, you can disagree with me as much as you like; it will be what you think about Jesus that matters. What I have written is simply to encourage you to take the story seriously and make it your own.

Let me begin at the beginning. There was always something about Jesus that 'got me' – something simple and direct and to the point. There was much in the gospels that mystified and puzzled me, and some things that were utterly obscure. I didn't know what to make of them, or how to relate them to those obvious convictions Jesus held and the plain way in which he lived. There are many things in his story I still don't understand and about which, if you asked me, I would just have to say 'I don't know'.

But I quickly found out that what was at the bottom of many of my difficulties was that I was reading the gospels – as I was reading the whole Bible – without any discrimination. I was reading it 'flat'. I owe to New Testament scholars and historians a great debt. They showed me that I must read these accounts of Jesus as I read other books, allow for different kinds of evidence, sort out what I was reading, remember what century Jesus was living in (I was reading him as if he were a twentieth-century contemporary of mine) and so take stock of him. I began to see him against the background of his own country and century. As I did so, he did not so much recede into the distance (as I thought he would) as stand out of his background and speak to me across the centuries in a language which I knew that I really understood and couldn't put on one side. I don't know that I was ever troubled by the fact that his view of the world and its history was very different from mine. 'What else do I expect', I remember saying to myself, 'if I am listening to someone in the first century talking?' And I learned, when I lived in North China, that you can live among people of another culture and way of thinking and speaking, and know what it is that they are really saying. I think I knew what Jesus was really saying, and while it seemed to clear my mind it made me uncomfortable and self-critical. There was an imperative note in his voice.

Two things opened my eyes and made the story of Jesus 'come home' to me. You will have seen already what these are by the way I have set his story out. I find it difficult to exaggerate the change it made in my thinking about him. The first was the discovery – and it was indeed a discovery to me – that he lived in an occupied country with its resistance movement. I had lived in Asia in such a country and knew what that was like. Suddenly, whatever I made of Jesus, I could never again think of him as a mere figure in the past or (as some of my friends seemed to think) as a teacher of pious platitudes. He stood for something that cost him his life, and I began to understand why the death of Jesus loomed so large in the thought and memory of his friends. It came then as no surprise to find how much of the gospels is concerned with this event. When I learned something more of what crucifixion actually meant in the ancient world and the horror of it – it was the ultimate punishment of slaves – and realised that Jesus faced it when he could have run away, I began to ask what it was he really stood for.

The second thing is something you mustn't smile about – it was a serious and fundamental discovery for me. I found out that Jesus was a poet – as indeed I had already found out that the Hebrew prophets were poets. This lifted an enormous weight from my shoulders and opened up for me vast horizons that I've never been able to reach. I do not mean that this discovery was simply a sort of 'literary' discovery. It was of course that. But it was much more. It meant that Jesus (if I may so put it) spoke to me differently. His demands were just as imperative as ever they were. But they came at me differently. They didn't shout at me; they fired my imagination. They put Jesus along with men and women of my own century who spoke directly to me, the poets and creative writers of my time, many of whom in the course of my lifetime were to find themselves in prison or exile or even facing death. I realised that what Jesus was giving me was a vision, a new experience. I understood, too, why Jesus is reported to have said 'I came to set the world on fire'.

What do poets have to say about themselves and their job in human society? Consider these quotations.

Milan Kundera, a Marxist writer from Czechoslovakia, showed what he thought a poet is doing when he said, at the Czech Writers' Fourth Conference in 1967, 'In our society it is considered a greater virtue to guard frontiers than to cross them'. In a study of Wordsworth, a poet is described as 'a man who throws stones at your window (if he is a poet of any power he breaks it)'. T. S. Eliot spoke of

> the intolerable wrestle
> with words and meanings.

Pablo Neruda (whose poem we quoted when we were talking about Jesus being a poet) described his 'job' as being

> to wake you up
> although you may not like it.

I began to think of Jesus as 'breaking windows', 'crossing frontiers', 'waking people up', getting words straight so that people can really talk to one another and make 'Yes' mean 'Yes' and 'No' mean 'No'.

What did Jesus begin to mean to me as I looked at him with fresh eyes?

Let me summarise it briefly.

The first thing that became clear to me was that Jesus was not just giving me orders, but drawing me into a discussion – as he drew so many people in his three brief years. He was raising questions and (what I found more disturbing) challenging the assumptions I was making in my own mind as he challenged the assumptions of his countrymen. He was forcing me to start my thinking all over again. It was when I realised that his stories and poems were opening a new world for me (they had been little more than moral illustrations) that I began to be aware that he was questioning the very basis of the world I had been living in so unconcernedly – even the 'Christian world' of church and home. Had I been so sure I knew what the answers were? Did I really understand the meaning of the words I was using? Did I really know what sort of world it was or ought to be?

Jesus came to me first of all, then, as my critic. I began to realise that the stories of how he criticised his friends (it must have cost them something to put those in) and his countrymen and the widely accepted human ways of going about things, were stories I had got to take seriously for myself: 'There go I'! So I began to discover that what Jesus meant to me was a call to explore this world in which I lived, and to face it – and myself – without pretence, as it really is. It was no Utopia Jesus was talking about.

It was then that the second thing became clear to me: in all this, I found that Jesus had made God real to me. I don't know how he did this. But I became profoundly aware that the world I was facing – with all its grave confusions – was God's world and was a world he was still making. Jesus did not talk about himself (it took me some time to get this clear); he talked about the job that God had given him to do and what God was like and what he was doing. He made it plain to me that the essential thing we've got to do if we're to make sense of this world (about which we all know very little indeed) and if we're to do something about it, was simply to take God at his word. That's what Jesus himself did. That's what I've got to do. And so, the greatest thing about Jesus for me was, as I have said, that he made God real. He didn't blow away all the mystery and strangeness; he didn't answer many of my questions. But he made God real to me – someone I had to say Yes or No to – and I knew what that Yes and No meant. In words I have read somewhere, he made 'goodness interesting'. I've never been bored since. If this is the truth about God and the world (summed up by Jesus in what we call the 'Lord's Prayer'), I've never understood how anybody could be bored. How could you be bored? Whoever you are, wherever you are, whatever job you've got, you know what you've to get on with – you are (in Paul's words) God's 'fellow-worker'. You've a world to explore and a job to do in it.

The third thing that became clear to me springs from what Jesus did. He made clear to me that the growing point of genuinely human society (call it 'God's Family' if you will) is what we do for the fellow who is left out of the picture, whom nobody bothers with, who doesn't seem to belong, who is 'out of it'. There can be no genuine human society if anybody is left out; if we leave anybody out we corrupt human society and destroy it. All this threw a new light for me on what, wherever I was, I ought to be concerned with; how I ought to look at whatever job I'd got (and where I should do it); and what I ought to press for, in every way I knew how, in the public life of the world. The growing points of my world were to be where people were ignored, forgotten or in need – people in prison for conscience' sake, people who were the victims of starvation and the injustices of a world divided up into the 'haves' and the have-nots'. It came home to me that what Jesus was talking about was not about just 'being kind' and 'generous', but about how a world can ever be a world in any worth-while sense of that word. When he talked about God being 'Father', he was not just saying something about God, he was making clear what for him made all the difference to the way he lived and the way we must all live. To talk about the world as 'God's Family' is not to dream of some distant future – it is to acknowledge the truth about the world where, here and now, I have got to live. We can have a *world* in no other way. When I pray the Lord's Prayer, I'm not just indulging in a pious but rather meaningless habit; I am accepting my marching orders.

And if ever I, for even one moment, thought that all this was easy or naïve, Jesus's death within three brief years as a threat to the Roman peace stabbed me wide awake.

It will now be clear that for me the first decisive fact about Jesus is his humanity. Whatever else he was, he was a real man.

We forget, as one of the great New Testament scholars of our time has put it, that 'in the earliest records Jesus is portrayed, not as the object of religion, but as a religious man'. Whatever else we may feel compelled to say about him we must hold fast to this. We must not belittle it or try to explain it away.

Jesus, as one of his early friends says 'was tested in every way as we are'. He had to face his world as we have to face ours and he had to come to his convictions as we have to come to ours. That is why what he did and said can speak to me, even after nearly two thousand years.

Jesus not only shared our human limitations, but he shared our ignorance. 'With all our learning,' as Paul said, 'we don't know very much.' Jesus shared the knowledge of his time, and had to learn, as we do, by trial and error. He could sometimes be wrong. He thought, for example, that his friends would stand by him, but they didn't. All this is what it means to be 'genuinely human'.

If, as in a moment, I have to go further and say more about Jesus than I have so far said, it will all rest upon this clear understanding that his story is a real story about a real man. That's where I begin.

I must now go further.

Jesus, as I have said, made God real for me. By that I mean more than that he 'helped me to think more clearly' about God. It is this something more I find very difficult to explain.

Let me take it step by step.

I mean by 'making God real' something more like 'helping me to be aware of God's presence'. Even here words are proving rather awkward, for by 'being aware of' I really mean more than 'feeling'; this experience touches not only my emotion but also my mind and my style of living – indeed, the whole of me.

This is something I have felt in the presence of deeply religious people, both Christian and those who are not Christian. I can think of a number of people (some of whom would be surprised to know that I am sitting in this room writing about them like this) who have made me feel God's presence – his nearness, his love and care and his power. I do not know how to describe this experience, but it is something that has been very important for me.

Now when I say that Jesus 'makes God real' for me, I mean that he has made possible a new experience of God and that this 'new experience' or 'new awareness' is not altogether different from the experiences I described in the last paragraph. Yet it is in some way unique. As someone has put it, 'when I think of Jesus I think of God; and when I think of God I think of Jesus'.

When I ask myself why this should be, I can only go back to the very first friends of Jesus and their 'new experience' of God. Their account of how they came to be aware of God in this new way strikes me as very near the truth for me. They held that God 'vindicated' Jesus (this is what we mean by 'the resurrection').

Now it seems to me that if all that Jesus stood for and all he was – his convictions about God and his trust in God – is anywhere near the truth of the matter, then it would be in God's nature to make it utterly plain that Jesus was right. For Jesus, God is Father and Creator. The world – the whole existing universe – is his world and he is still at work in it; it is his family in the making. It is a world in which we are free to say Yes or No, for God wants free men and women, not automata, as members of his family. His purpose from the very beginning was the making of a worthwhile world in which men and women 'might grow up to be the kind of person Jesus was, so that Jesus might be the elder brother of a great family of brothers and sisters'. The story of Jesus could not, therefore, just peter out.

I know that this is talking about God as though he were another person like ourselves, and that he is not 'another person like ourselves', but the source and ground of all that is. But we have to use our ordinary language and our ordinary experience if we are to talk at all about him; and here Paul's words, which I have just quoted, seem to be better at saying what I want to say than any other words I know.

This great act on God's part of 'making clear that Jesus was right' ('vindicating' him) is, as I have just said, what Christians have called his 'resurrection'. We have seen what Jesus's first friends had to say about this. If my experience of God here and now in this twentieth century as I have described it is to be explained for me, I cannot but think that Jesus's first friends' claim about what happened must be near the truth. God's act in 'vindicating' Jesus made possible a new experience of God. It made clear that God's love is the power that is making and sustaining the universe and that God is not some remote power but a presence in our hearts.

All this does not mean that God has only one way to speak to us. He is present everywhere in all men's hearts and in the whole of human history. Therefore, if God is 'Father' as Jesus made plain and if he has made it clear that Jesus was right (as his first friends affirmed), I must be open to all truth however and by whomsoever it is discovered. I must be ready to listen as well as talk with all sincere people whoever they may be and I must be ready to share with others all that Jesus means to me.

It doesn't surprise me that men and women have many different experiences of God, many different ways of looking at the world, many different 'awarenesses' of God. It doesn't surprise me, either, that the friends of Jesus themselves have differed among themselves in the ways they think about God, worship him and work out their common life. All this is what I would expect to find in God's world where we are at the very beginning of discovering its range and richness, and where, in Paul's words, 'neither dying nor living, neither what we're facing now nor what we may have to face tomorrow, nothing in our own world or in outer space or in our own hearts can take away from us God's love'.

And for me, it is Jesus – in the way he lived, in the way he died and in the new experience of God that he made possible – who makes me quite certain that all this is on the right track.

I know that Christians have said many things, used many words, given Jesus many titles to try to explain all this. They are not agreed among themselves and the debate about all that Jesus means is as lively today as ever it was. All this too does not surprise me – I would be surprised if it were not so. I shall not deal with all this 'special talk' here. I am only concerned to show the direction in which I have found I must walk if I take seriously all that Jesus means to me. Your way may be very different from mine. That is your business and I wish you well.

I can only say, to put where I stand briefly, that Jesus has meant for me a new experience of God, a new awareness of the worthwhileness of the world (with all its mystery and in spite of all its evil) and a new sense of who I am. And all this in this very different twentieth century. He has put the clue in my hands and made the world a marvellous and exciting place to be alive in – as exciting now as it became when I first began to grasp what he could really mean. How could it be otherwise if the world is what Jesus believed it to be – God his Father's world?

And you can see, too, why I've got to be in the community he began. If he was right, there can be no standing on the touchline.

I have two convictions to add. What I have so far said would be incomplete without them. They are convictions that have grown stronger as I've grown older.

The first is this. I have talked about God 'vindicating' Jesus, 'making it plain that Jesus is right'. It is this (however difficult to put into words) that makes the story of Jesus for me, as I have said, something much more than a story of something that happened in the past. The death of Jesus, from one point of view, was a tragedy, symbolising all the suffering and evil in the world and that contempt of all we know to be good of which we are all capable. If that were all to be said, the world for me would be a senseless, meaningless and cruel place. I don't think that the word 'God' would mean anything at all to me – I certainly couldn't 'believe' in him. But the fact that I can see God sharing the suffering and evil, dealing with it in all its horror and defeating it, helps me to see all our human experience as meaningful and worthwhile, even though its suffering and evil leave me still bewildered. The very word 'cross' – a dreadful word – changes its meaning. It stands – if God 'vindicated' Jesus as I believe he did – for the length to which God is prepared to go, and it makes 'love' a real and not a glib word. I think I can begin to understand why Paul said he could 'boast' in the cross.

The second conviction is this. When I first began to grasp what Jesus stood for, I was filled with immense hope. It was hope for the world – suffering and evil were not the last word. It was a hope that turned death from an end of everything to a beginning. It was hope, not just for the world in general, but for individual men and women – for me. What Jesus meant when he talked of 'God's Day' and of 'God's Rule' were no idle words. Everything – this world and whatever world lies beyond it – is in God my Father's hands. I can get on with whatever job I've got to do and leave the rest to him.

Doesn't that make sense?

Index to quotations from the Bible

This index will help you not only to track down the quotations from the Bible I have used, but also to go further in examining the story of Jesus. It is important to read passages from the gospels against their background and setting (why did the early friends of Jesus choose just this story to remember?) and as Mark and Luke and Matthew have actually used them in the making of their books. This index will help you to find the setting and arrangement they have been given. In *Winding Quest* and *New World*, I have arranged material from both the Old Testament and the New Testament in the light of the work of historians and Bible scholars; it will help you to see where I have put a passage I have quoted and how I have arranged it there.

NOTE: M = Matthew; Mk = Mark; L = Luke; J = John. The second page number given in brackets for *New World* refers to the first edition. All references are to *New World* unless otherwise stated. WQ = *Winding Quest*.

Index of Bible References

NOTE: Numbers in italics refer to page references in this book.

Index of Other References

See Acknowledgments, p.x, for abbreviations

Index of Jesus's Parables and Poems

Index of Subjects